W9-DJK-283

Your Career in

ART AND DESIGN

by

Carolyn Hawes
Rhode Island School of Design

Margaret Johnson
Massachusetts College of Art

Judith Nylen
Pratt Institute

ARCO PUBLISHING COMPANY, INC.
219 Park Avenue South, New York, N.Y. 10003

Dedicated to our alumni who so generously shared their career paths and expertise with us.

Second Printing, 1978
Published by Arco Publishing Company, Inc.
219 Park Avenue South, New York, N.Y. 10003

Library of Congress Cataloging in Publication Data

Hawes, Carolyn.
Your career in art and design.

Bibliography: p. 145
1. Art—Vocational guidance. I. Johnson, Margaret, 1923- joint author. II. Nylen, Judith, joint author. III. Title.

N8350.H38 700'.23 76-41912
ISBN 0-668-04141-2 (Paper Edition)

Printed in the United States of America

Contents

CHAPTER I

Choosing an Art Career

If you do not have artistic talent, read no further because artists do not choose an art career, it usually chooses them. You may choose to attend art school, a university with an art department, or study independently, but your talent is innate, and you come into this life already endowed with it. From the earliest moments you were motivated to draw, use crayons, caricature your teachers, work in clay, make a table or cut on it while being lectured to. When you had to stay in on rainy days it was never as bad for you because there was always a pad and pencil somewhere. If you had understanding parents, or only one understanding parent, an encouraging teacher, or an interested friend, you were way ahead.

But what are you? You are a creative problem solver who will face a myriad of problems—the problems you want to solve on paper or canvas, in bronze, with clay, or by weaving—and your relation to the society which does not understand what you are doing in that space, with that form, or to that design, and how it is going to effect them anyway.

So, being committed to your talents is not enough. You have to meet and deal with people, and you have to be able to communicate verbally as well as visually. Artists/designers are no longer elitist; they are in the mainstream of society. It is not a case of being wanted or appreciated for your gifts; it is a case of being needed. Pure and simple—your next choice is selection of a career path.

In choosing your career path you will have to decide whether to become a designer or a fine artist. The difference between the two is that designers and craftspersons prepare for a career so that their talent will support them, and fine artists often work to support their careers. Both are two- and three-dimensional problem solvers and both satisfy creative goals. Aesthetically the designer is more interested in the traditional or utilitarian, whereas the fine artist deals with the interpretive. There can, of course, be overlapping: designers who pot, paint, and sculpt and ceramists, painters, and sculptors who design products and make crafts. In making this choice you eventually will have to deal with your goals and your sensitivities, knowing that design is more practical than fine arts.

To select a school or college or university, we suggest you use the *American Art Directory*, published by R. R. Bowker Co., 1180 Avenue of the Americas, New York, N.Y. 10036, which lists alphabetically by state the kinds of schools with their major programs, the names and addresses of the deans or directors, financial aid programs, and kinds of degrees. Writing for a catalog is your best way of obtaining information and visiting a school is your best way of gaining insight into its program.

At the end of the book is a list of directories and publications which may be helpful to you in learning about specific programs, reading about individual fields, and gathering additional information. If your local and school libraries do not have them, they can be ordered by writing to the addresses given. Some of the directories are costly for individual purchases, and some of the magazines are issued only for professionals in the field. The latter, however, are excellent sources of up-to-date activities within a field and often give real insight to the young person contemplating a career choice. Employment trends and basic opportunities continually change, and it is through the professional publications that these activities are identified.

The following professional organizations may be helpful to you in answering questions about opportunities in their fields.

Advertising Club of New York
23 Park Avenue
New York, N.Y. 10016

American Crafts Council
44 West 53rd Street
New York, N.Y. 10019

American Institute of Architects (in most large cities)
National Chapter
1735 New York Avenue, NW
Washington, D.C. 20006

American Institute of Graphic Arts
1059 Third Avenue
New York, N.Y. 10021

American Society of Interior Designers
730 Fifth Avenue
New York, N.Y. 10022

American Society of Magazine Photographers
60 East 42nd Street
New York, N.Y. 10017

The American Theatre Society, Inc.
226 West 47th Street
New York, N.Y. 10036

Art Directors Clubs (in most large cities)
488 Madison Avenue
New York, N.Y. 10022

College Art Association
16 East 52nd Street
New York, N.Y. 10022

Package Designers Council
619 Second Avenue
New York, N.Y. 10016

Point of Purchase Advertising Institute
60 East 42nd Street
New York, N.Y. 10036

Society of Illustrators
128 East 63rd Street
New York, N.Y. 10021

Society of Photographer and Artist Representatives, Inc.
Box 845
New York, N.Y. 10022

Through your entire college years utilize your Career Planning Office to find assistance in your choice of career paths and to learn the kinds of opportunities for employment in the current market. In this office also, you will find part-time and summer jobs to help supplement the cost of your education.

CHAPTER II

Architecture

If you like building with blocks and thinking in terms of who will live in, work in, or worship in a building, you may want to consider becoming an architect—the artist of the technical professions and the technician of the artistic professions. The design of human spaces and the systems which interconnect them is your essential function as architect and planner. Combined with these talents you must have the ability to meet and deal with people because not only will you deal with clients and colleagues, you will need to assess zoning laws; to be aware of the needs of the individuals occupying your building; to talk with lawyers and real estate brokers; to know the language of the engineer, construction boss, and laborer; and to be sensitive to the effect your design will have on the whole community.

Education

Your education may be at the Bachelor's level, a five-year program leading to the Bachelor of Architecture degree, or, after four years of college and receipt of a B.A. or B.S. degree, on to a Master's program offering a first professional degree. Your study of architectural design will involve the correlation of structural, functional, and behavioral information as well as drafting, rendering, and graphic presentation. Your courses will include two- and three-dimensional design, perspective drawing, use of tools, strengths of materials, structures, history of architecture, and other technically related subjects. Along

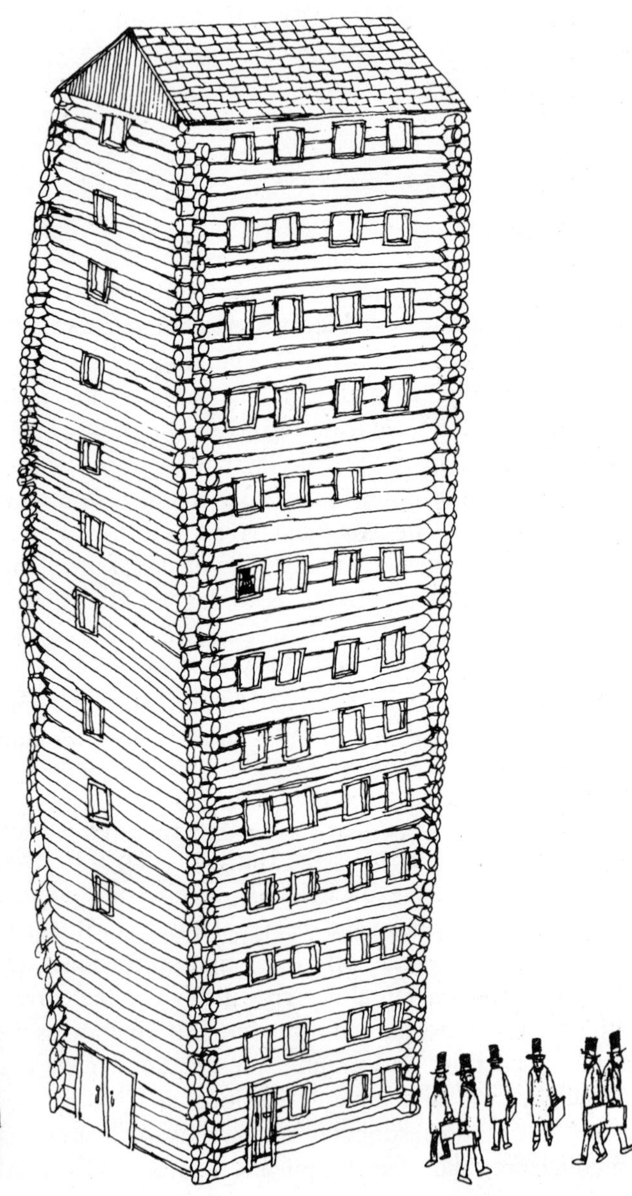

with these requirements electives in photography, graphic design, community planning, and crafts can be very useful. Any liberal arts subjects, especially those that deal with communication skills, can aid you as you pursue your career.

Particularly helpful is the critique of your work when a project is completed. This is made by a jury composed of visiting professionals and your faculty, who are usually practicing architects themselves. During these critiques you will have the opportunity to defend your design choices and solutions much as you are required to do with clients when you are practicing architecture.

Related Areas

In architecture there are related areas which the trained architect may enter, such as:

City and Regional Planning—design of specifically designated areas, concerned with public, commercial, and transportation space organization;
Urban Renewal—improving an urban area by design, building, landscape, layout, lighting, etc.;
Restoration/Preservation—improving and maintaining an old building and sometimes an old city;
Transportation Systems—studying and improving ways and means of people moving from place to place;
Interior Architecture—planning and designing internal space;
Landscape Architecture—designing terrain and planning the natural surroundings, after preserving natural resources.

The latter two are professions unto themselves and have specific related degree requirements. They often work for and with architects in planning and implementing architectural commissions.

After Graduation

The largest number of graduates will enter architectural firms, large and small, where they will become involved in work for many different kinds of clients—e.g., industries and businesses building new corporations; builders and planners creating new neighborhoods; families planning new houses; educational institutions expanding or planning new facilities; hospitals and churches seeking additions or new structures. Some graduates will enter corporations—oil companies, supermarkets, hotels, and a few large industrial complexes—which have an in-house architect to administer their long-range building programs that may involve both national and international expansion. Others will work for the federal, state, and local governments which are among the most prodigious of builders, both at home and abroad. These projects can range from a simple edifice to an entire complex encompassing a whole city. Because architecture is a profession, like medicine or law, a Civil Service examination is not generally required. However, state laws regulate the right to practice architecture, beginning with a requirement of a "first professional degree" from an accredited school of architecture. These laws vary among states, which makes it imperative that an architect be familiar with the legal requirements of a particular state prior to proceeding with an architectural project. Upon receiving your B. Arch. degree and looking toward registration, you should write to the National Council of Architectural Registration Boards, 521 18th Street, N.W., Washington, D.C., to determine the prerequisites necessary to become a registered architect.

After You Are Hired

Don't be surprised if you feel like a "go for," because your beginning job will pretty much keep you at the drawing board drafting, reworking plans, sketching, detailing, and interpreting line drawings. Larger offices lean towards specialization, where you may become involved exclusively with doors and windows; smaller offices may offer more diversity but not the opportunity to work on the larger complexes. In either case, actual designing may be a few years away, and attaining that position will require a willingness to share in the teamwork and to recognize that there are many steps between concept and implementation. There are even those within a firm who will lean towards model making, graphic design, photography, supervising, specification and program writing (analyzing items and materials which go into a structure), and personnel. A few individuals may become architectural critics and historians, and a number may enter teaching, primarily at the post-secondary level, while continuing to practice.

Restoration has become an increasingly popular specialization, because the preserving of old structures seems to be replacing the building of new ones. This requires both historical accuracy and contemporary technical construction techniques and is an area which needs the combined thinking of the architect, interior architect, and landscape architect to come off with conviction.

The Years Ahead

The massive building programs of the fifties and sixties do not seem likely to continue into the future, and there will be those architects who, though well-educated in their field, must think of alternative job choices. Possibilities lie in any area using three-dimensional design, such as industrial design, interior design, graphic design, the construction industry, furniture design, toy design, lighting design, packaging design, exhibit design, textile design (woven), and the like.

Professional journals and magazines can be of assistance to

Architecture Career Paths

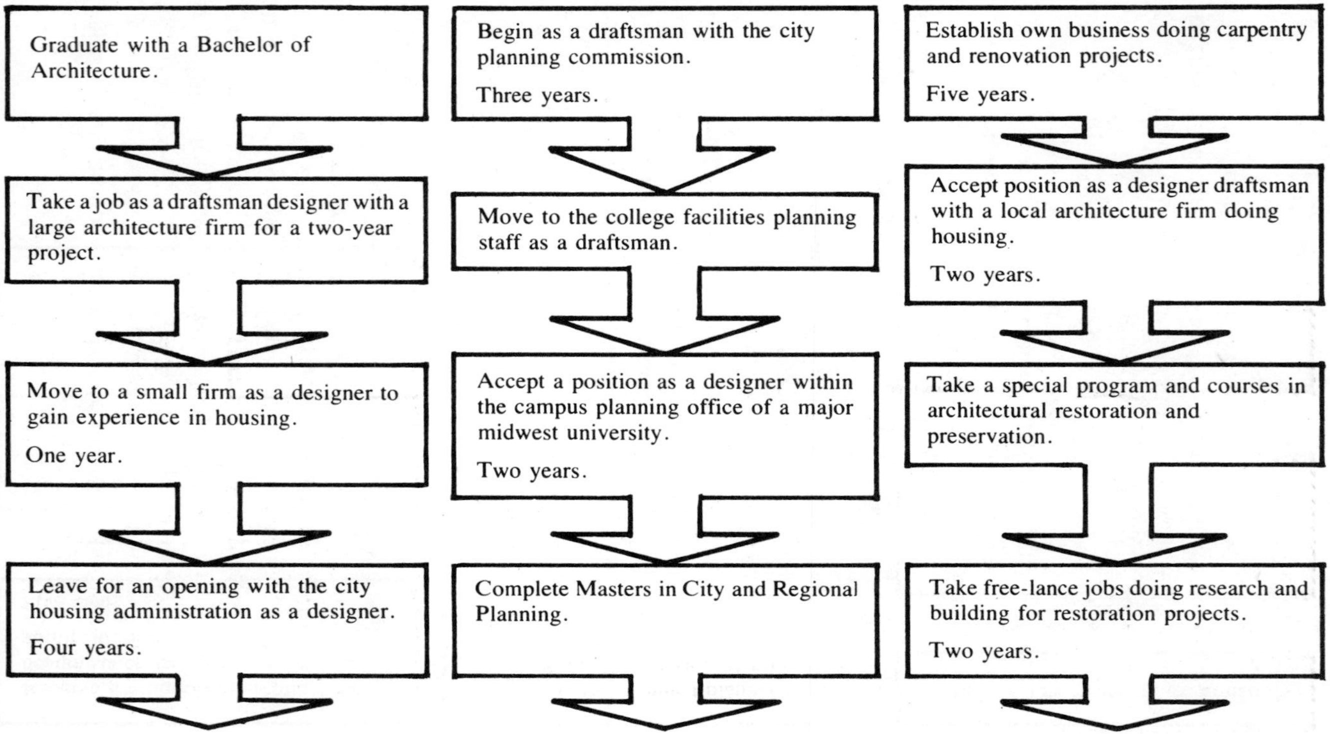

Graduate with a Bachelor of Architecture.

Take a job as a draftsman designer with a large architecture firm for a two-year project.

Move to a small firm as a designer to gain experience in housing.

One year.

Leave for an opening with the city housing administration as a designer.

Four years.

Begin as a draftsman with the city planning commission.

Three years.

Move to the college facilities planning staff as a draftsman.

Accept a position as a designer within the campus planning office of a major midwest university.

Two years.

Complete Masters in City and Regional Planning.

Establish own business doing carpentry and renovation projects.

Five years.

Accept position as a designer draftsman with a local architecture firm doing housing.

Two years.

Take a special program and courses in architectural restoration and preservation.

Take free-lance jobs doing research and building for restoration projects.

Two years.

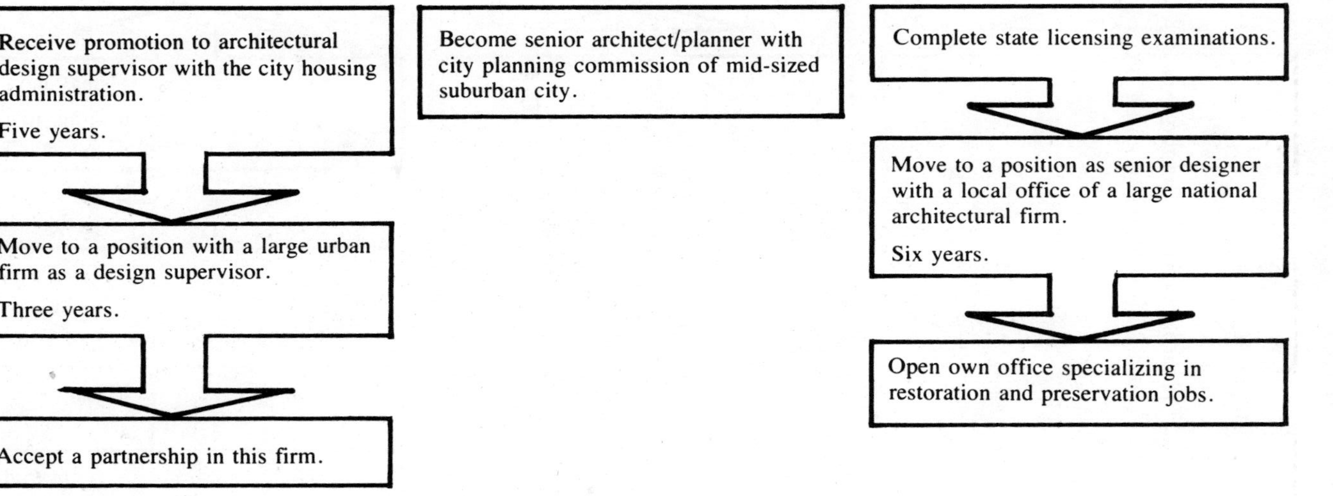

Receive promotion to architectural design supervisor with the city housing administration.
Five years.
Move to a position with a large urban firm as a design supervisor.
Three years.
Accept a partnership in this firm.
Become senior architect/planner with city planning commission of mid-sized suburban city.
Complete state licensing examinations.
Move to a position as senior designer with a local office of a large national architectural firm.
Six years.
Open own office specializing in restoration and preservation jobs.

you in making your plans and in learning more about the field. To help you here, there is a list of publications beginning on page 154.

CHAPTER III

Environmental Design

The design of interior spaces is generally the province of the environmental or interior designer for whom there are a variety of designations—environmental designer, interior designer, interior architect, space planner—but the primary function of the designer is to plan interior spaces, their construction, color, texture, and furnishing. The only distinction which might be made between the various "titles" applied to this field is between the designer and the decorator. The interior decorator usually concentrates on the furnishings and coloring of rooms while the designer is normally trained in and concerned with the visualization of the total space, its usage and construction, as well as color and furnishing. A further, but not necessarily exclusive, distinction is that the decorator is concerned with residential spaces while the interior designer or space planner deals with commercial spaces such as offices, banks, schools, restaurants, hospitals. Only a few interior designers have chosen to specialize in traditional or period design applied in commercial spaces while most qualified decorators are conversant with various period furnishings and appearances.

Education

If you are exploring a career in interior design, you will first need to consider whether your interests lie in decorating or design and choose the appropriate professional school to pursue your training. Beyond the normal curriculum, you may want to

consider course work in business management or in allied areas such as textile design, furniture design, graphic design, or exhibition design.

After Graduation

A career in the interiors field usually involves working with a team as a junior designer, in a design department in a retail store, a design studio, or in a consulting firm.

After You Are Hired

You will probably begin in the commercial field, as a draftsperson or an assistant to a designer collecting and filing copies of furniture and fabric samples and helping with presentation development. As you progress you will gradually become involved with the many aspects of design, including furniture design, fabric and color specification, which may include signage or super graphics, and with space planning. Most professional designers seem to agree that when hiring a young designer, they look for the ability to visualize space, to draft, to render, to be knowledgeable about construction methods, and to be aware of furniture and fabric trends and sources.

The Years Ahead

The field of interior design has been expanding over the past two decades and, in terms of the design of commercial spaces, has developed a professional standard similar to that in the architectural field. The decrease in the construction of new buildings in the United States indicates that many commercial firms and public institutions are choosing to renovate existing spaces when considering expansion or change. This task of refurbishing is generally the province of the interior designer

Environmental Design Career Paths

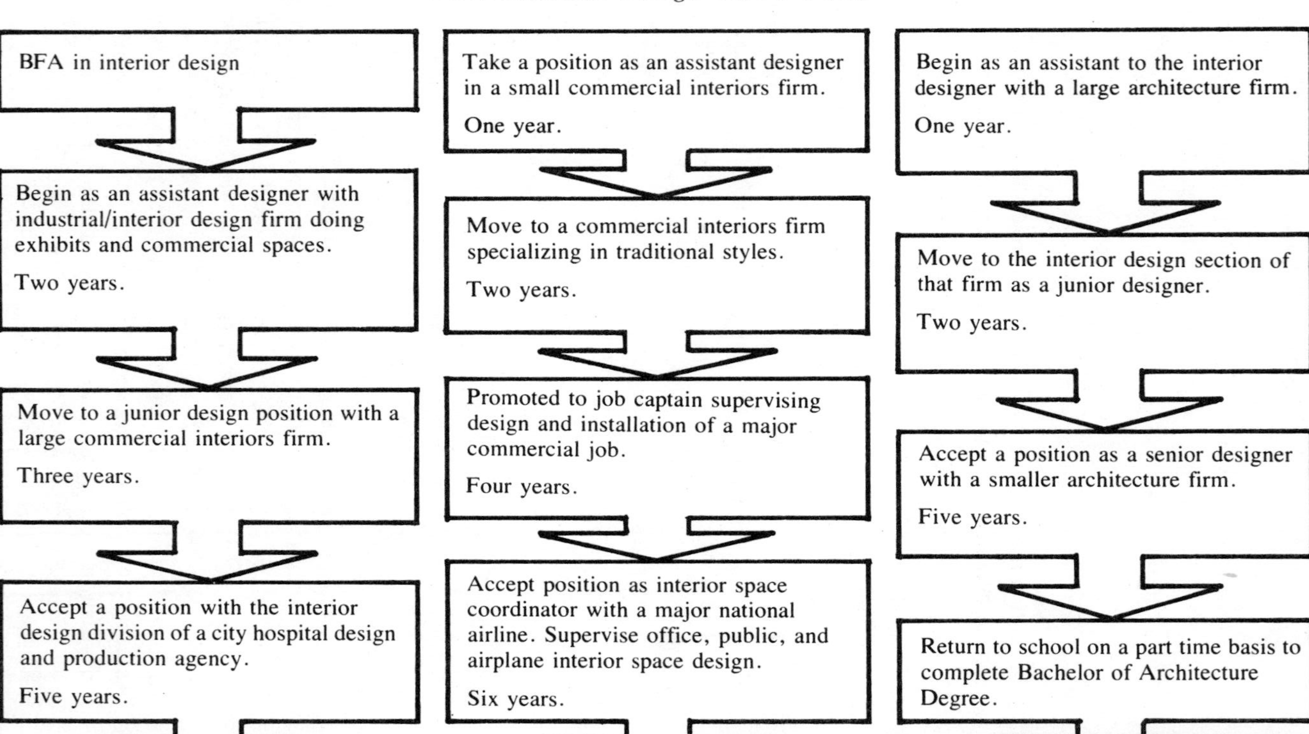

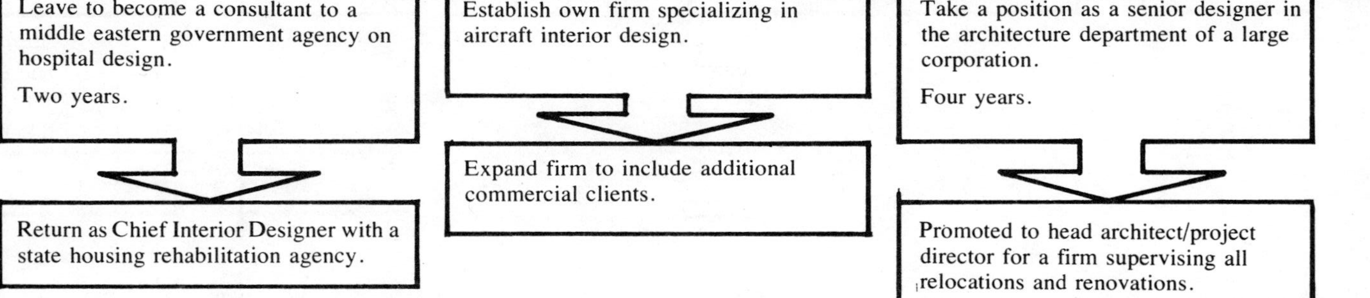
Leave to become a consultant to a middle eastern government agency on hospital design.
Two years.
Return as Chief Interior Designer with a state housing rehabilitation agency.
Establish own firm specializing in aircraft interior design.
Expand firm to include additional commercial clients.
Take a position as a senior designer in the architecture department of a large corporation.
Four years.
Promoted to head architect/project director for a firm supervising all relocations and renovations.

although there are architects who are becoming increasingly involved in interior space planning. In the future, interior designers, like architects, may be seeking career opportunities in allied fields.

CHAPTER IV

Industrial Design

The industrial designer combines technical knowledge of methods, materials, and machines with design talent to create and to improve the appearance and function of machine-made products. Industrial design is the design of the things you use every day: consumer products, transportation, computer products, industrial machinery, medical and hospital equipment, furniture, etc. Along with product design, an industrial designer may design packages, containers, transportation vehicles and systems; work on exhibits or displays; and act as a consultant to the medical profession where the continual improvement in instruments and the creation of apparatus requires special knowledge and training. It is in the intermediary process between industry and the consumer that industrial designers will use their expertise to design and refine products for efficient manufacture and consumer satisfaction.

Good design has been responsible for much of the economic and cultural rise in the contemporary standard of living. The impact of high quality design in everyday life has only been felt for about the last thirty-five years. It is now no longer exclusively for the wealthy but is available to people of middle and lower incomes as well. Today the industrial designer is becoming increasingly involved in the social sciences, particularly in education and welfare, where he may contribute to the design of abstract systems and the methods of teaching or disseminating information. It is important enough for governments of many

countries to institute tax supported "Design Councils" to encourage and finance quality design.

Education

The possibilities for a career in Industrial Design are growing every day. The qualities which will make you successful in this area are a combination of things: intelligence, a strong creative urge, curiosity, a desire to solve problems, a knowledge of technical and mechanical techniques, and an interest in people. You will usually work as a member of a team and, therefore, should be able to communicate your ideas well, both verbally and visually, by means of drawings and models. Because you are part designer, part technical person, and part merchandiser you will be considered a multi-disciplined person who must understand other areas of design. If possible you should have: skills in drafting, rendering, and model making; technical knowledge of materials, processes, and human engineering; aesthetic sensitivity to form, color, and composition. You should be aware of new ideas, trends, materials, processes, and equipment and new applications, for success develops through hard work and discipline.

In choosing your college program in industrial design it is a good idea to plan a program with sufficient opportunity for interchange with other design disciplines, namely: graphic design, photography, architecture, illustration, interior design, and space planning. It is also good, if time permits, to develop a working knowledge in crafts such as the materials and techniques used in glass, wood, metal, ceramics, sculpture, and textiles. This type of interdisciplinary learning tends to make you more creative and gives you greater breadth in your problem solving resources.

Industrial Design Career Paths

Begin as a designer technician with a large corporation, doing production drawing, drafting, presentations and some design as part of the design team

Four years.

Move to a large urban firm, working on product development and styling.

Six years.

Become a senior designer with a major corporation, supervising product design staff.

Two years.

Move to Europe as a Chief Designer for the European product market.

Three years.

Take a job as office boy and model maker for a well-known furniture designer.

One year.

Free-lance as an exhibit designer and modelmaker doing small exhibitions for educational institutions.

Four years.

Become Design Director for a specialty museum, developing on-going exhibition spaces and changing exhibits.

Eight years.

Form own consulting firm specializing in exhibition and interior space design. Concerned primarily with client contact and business administration, supervising design staff of 3.

Six years.

Take a position as an assistant designer in a consulting firm doing presentation drawing and prototypes for product development.

Three years.

Move to a small interior design and furniture firm as a junior designer, concentrating mainly on prototypes for furniture.

Five years.

Travel to Europe, marketing designs to manufacturers. Sell one chair design which goes into production.

Two years.

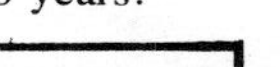

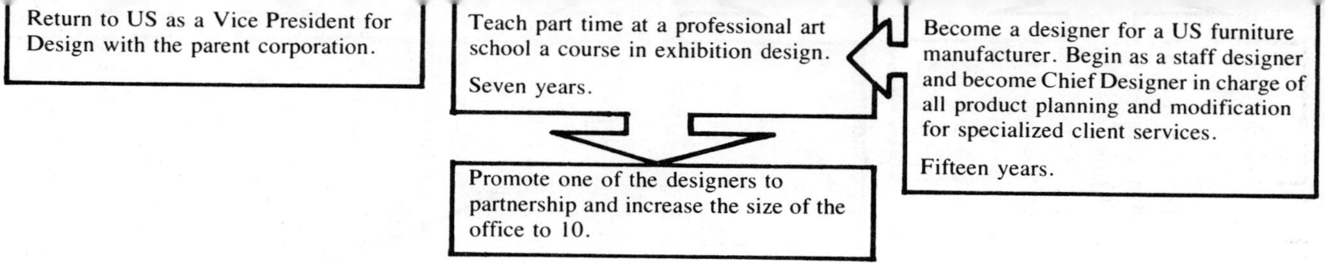

Return to US as a Vice President for Design with the parent corporation.

Teach part time at a professional art school a course in exhibition design.

Seven years.

Become a designer for a US furniture manufacturer. Begin as a staff designer and become Chief Designer in charge of all product planning and modification for specialized client services.

Fifteen years.

Promote one of the designers to partnership and increase the size of the office to 10.

After Graduation

For the industrial designer your career directions are diversified. You may make contact with design consulting firms, large manufacturing firms, large architectural firms, and the state and national governments. To begin your work experience while in school, you may want to explore opportunities by seeking part-time and/or summer employment in an industrial design office. If you have a chance to take industrial arts, such as mechanical drawing and shop training and creative art courses, before commitment to an industrial design area, do so. This will help to determine your ability and give you additional know-how. You will want to learn about the consumer and your fellow man.

After You Are Hired

In your beginning job you usually start out as an assistant to other designers, sometimes as model maker or draftsperson. If fortunate, you may start out as a junior designer and be included in the actual design process. With further experience, you will move into the design team as a full-fledged designer engaged in long-range planning and development of new products. A position in a design consulting firm will give you experience in different areas in addition to exposure to business procedures. In a staff design position in a corporation you have the added advantage of close communication with the engineering and marketing departments and the sales personnel during design conferences. Until you have gained considerable experience it is not advisable to free-lance, since the complexities of design, development, and production are fairly critical.

The Years Ahead

Uniqueness is what separates recognized designers from just plain designers, and those who are recognized are those who publish, speak, teach, and compete. They receive grants; they are asked to experiment, to explore, to present ideas to knowledgeable groups; they are aware of function and aesthetics; and they are innovative, creative, and have a knowledge of business acumen. You will be all of these things if designing is a way of life to you, and you can make this way of life understood by those with whom you associate professionally. It does not necessarily mean making a better mousetrap; it may mean dispensing with the need to make mousetraps at all.

CHAPTER V

Crafts

Craftspersons have a unique combination of skills in marketing, business and production, and fine arts. They may create one-of-a-kind pieces which will be directed toward the fine arts marketplace and simultaneously develop a line to sell to various shops or retail in his or her own shop or mail order business. Crafts signify a very special world of work: that of the "cottage industry" where the craftsperson "manufactures," markets, and sells work on a limited production basis. This world of work is particularly attractive because of the life style popularly associated with the craftsperson. However, do not mistake it for a life of leisure: crafts require much hard work with very low financial return. Although other designers and artists have on occasion elected to work in a style similar to that of the craftsperson, the crafts have traditionally involved ceramics, weaving, glass, fabric, jewelry, and wood pieces which fulfill a useful as well as aesthetic function.

Education

Your interest in crafts may have begun early in your schooling, and you may have even entered crafts fairs while still in high school. However, to become a professional person it is going to be to your advantage to attend a university, college or art school which has a good crafts program. You will need to learn to blow glass, build and fire a kiln, work various looms, melt metal, use hand power tools, tan leather, plus drawing, two- and three-dimensional design, and any painting or sculpture you care to elect. Liberal arts subjects add to making you a better educated person.

Because as a craftsperson you may become involved in the operation of a small business, it would seem essential that courses in marketing and accounting would be not only useful, but, very early in your career, a necessity. Beyond these two areas, perhaps some specific attention to market research and public relations would be helpful.

After Graduation

The career path for the craftsperson is one of slow growth as an artist. Most people involved in crafts must be prepared to make an initial investment of funds both in the "tools of the trade" and in promotion materials. The greatest investment, however, will be in personal time. Assuming this kind of commitment, you can begin to realize a profit, having covered initial outlay and overhead, in three to five years. This may seem like a long time, but you must consider that during this period you are immersed in your own creative development, an involvement common to artists and designers in their early years.

The craftsperson's first guideword is expertise. The major concern is the development of technical excellence. The distributors of your work are interested in seeing competently finished pieces which can be reproduced and will sell well. The second guideword is function. Although you may create nonfunctional one-of-a-kind pieces, the primary market will be the utilitarian objects to be sold to the consumer market.

Since craftspeople can be involved with both direct marketing and the production of pieces for exhibition in the fine arts marketplace, you must consider the requirements for presentation of each situation separately. For the "crafts" market, you will be developing a body of work which is at least in function repeatable. The potter may have a line which includes mugs, bowls, dinnerware sets, bottles, jars, and casseroles; the weaver may develop wall hangings, pillows, apparel fabric, rugs, or bedspreads; the jeweler may have bracelets, rings, necklaces, and earrings. Most shops handling the work of craftspeople will want to see your best samples, sometimes in the original, sometimes in slides or color photographs. You must be prepared to quote wholesale prices which you can deliver within agreed-upon deadlines. Most shopowners will need a 30 day billing period, but many craftspeople offer 10 percent discount for invoices paid in less than 30 days. Very few outlets are able to pay at the time of delivery and almost never in advance. The craftsperson is generally responsible for delivery or shipping and must consider this in developing an arrangement with outlets.

After You Are Hired

Occasionally there is an apprenticeship whereby you learn many tricks of the trade as well as having an opportunity to see that there is a business aspect to this profession. Because most craftspeople work independently, they are generally hired during the busy season, often directly upon graduation from school.

The Years Ahead

With the increasing interest and acceptance of crafts in the world of fine arts, the craftsperson has opportunities to exhibit and sell work through major galleries and museums, several of which have emerged which specialize in crafts. Major museums have begun to include fiber, ceramic, glass, and wood work in their sculpture and painting collections as well as under the "applied" arts. However, the guiding principle is usually work

Crafts Career Paths

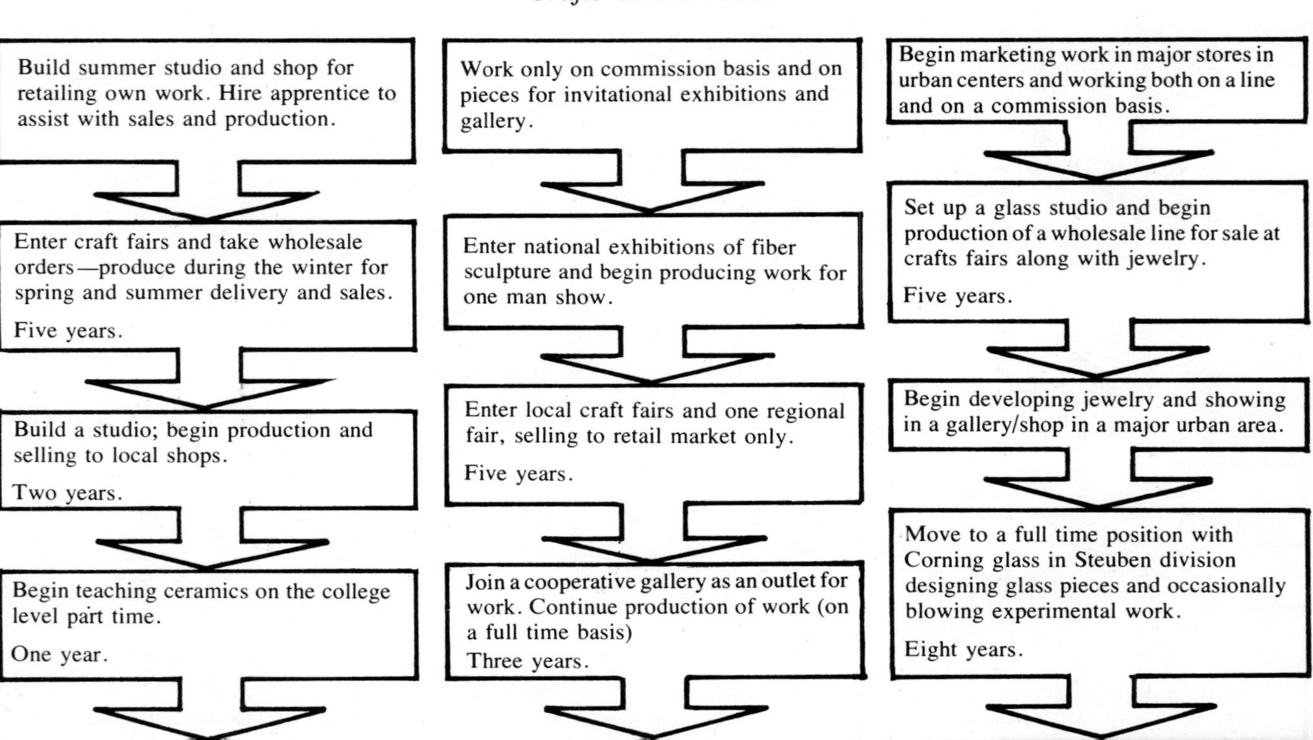

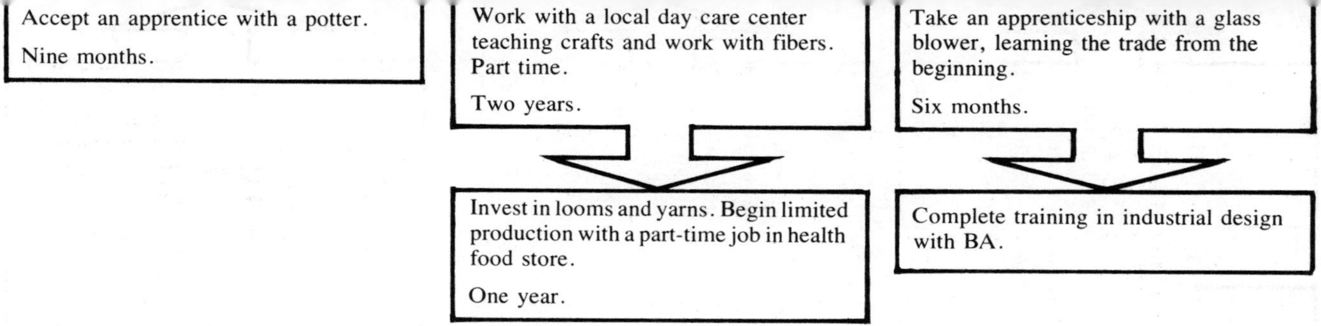

Accept an apprentice with a potter.

Nine months.

Work with a local day care center teaching crafts and work with fibers. Part time.

Two years.

Invest in looms and yarns. Begin limited production with a part-time job in health food store.

One year.

Take an apprenticeship with a glass blower, learning the trade from the beginning.

Six months.

Complete training in industrial design with BA.

which is one-of-a-kind and involved more with aesthetic than functional concepts. If you are developing work of this nature, you should refer to the section on fine arts and explore the path to a career as a professional exhibiting artist.

Setting prices, wholesale, retail, and for exhibition, is perhaps your most difficult task, especially early in your career. Retail outlets are interested in work which is consistent in price with other work they handle and competitive with neighboring shops. Until you have become accustomed to production work, you may find that your time is costly. However, once your initial investments have been covered, you will begin to earn a living wage, providing you remain professional about the production and marketing of your work.

The crafts have been a growing market for the past ten years, as the consumer increasingly looks for well-made, well-designed products which will last. This presents a hopeful picture for you as a craftsperson if you have the energy and dedication required. Some consideration must be given to the locale in which you choose to work since many areas are becoming saturated while others are essentially unused. Constant contact with both the American Crafts Council and any local crafts organizations will give you access to information about fairs, shows, and related work opportunities.

CHAPTER VI

Apparel Design

Being an apparel designer conjures up a vision of working in a well-known design house, for a well-known designer on one-of-a-kind haute couture basis. In reality, it may mean selling ready-to-wear in a local department store. However, in between are hundreds of things you can do, and to do them, you will want to think first about your education and then your job hunting.

Education

You may wish to attend an art school which offers an apparel design program leading to a BFA degree or you may choose to take a non-degree program in a school specializing in fashion design. Whichever you choose, you will want a thorough grounding in drawing, two- and three-dimensional design, color theory, design and utilization of fabrics, draping, fashion illustration, pattern making, silk screening, and history of costume. Any liberal arts subjects will be helpful to you because you will be meeting and dealing with people, and in almost any job today you need to be able to use and understand words.

While you are in school any fashion shows you can attend or participate in will be to your advantage, and to be familiar with the current fashion magazines and publications is expected of you. One thing you want to remember is that you should not be keeping up with the current fashions, you should be ahead of them, both in design and the use of color and fabric.

After Graduation

If you want to be a designer in a well-known house, New York City has more of these than any other city. Although Boston, Detroit, Kansas City, Chicago, and San Francisco may offer good experiences for a beginner, New York City is where most of the leading designers work and produce. And to get a job in one of these houses you have to hustle, be competitive (a strong back and a hard head), and be able to think on your feet while creating in your mind. If you catch on and can take the pace . . . no problem. But getting the first job may be, for this means having a top notch portfolio with diversified designs plus a willingness to do menial tasks to get your foot in the door. After that you're on your own.

Supposing you choose not to go to New York City, London, or Paris, where then? Smaller cities do have some established design houses. For instance, there are houses for sportswear in Boston, children's wear in Chicago, sports and beachwear in Los Angeles, men's wear in Kansas City. These are primarily traditional houses creating variations on a theme. If it is not creative enough you can always do your own designing on your own time, and maybe even set up a part-time studio of your own, or find an agent who is willing to sell the apparel you design and produce.

The Years Ahead

You may want to think of alternative jobs involving the apparel industry, such as merchandising or retailing, where you can enter a training program with a department store for a specified period at the end of which time you become an assistant buyer, and as openings occur move on to a buyer, a fashion coordinator, or a fashion consultant, utilizing accessories as well as apparel. Stores offering this kind of opportunity exist all over the country in almost every medium-size or

Apparel Design Career Paths

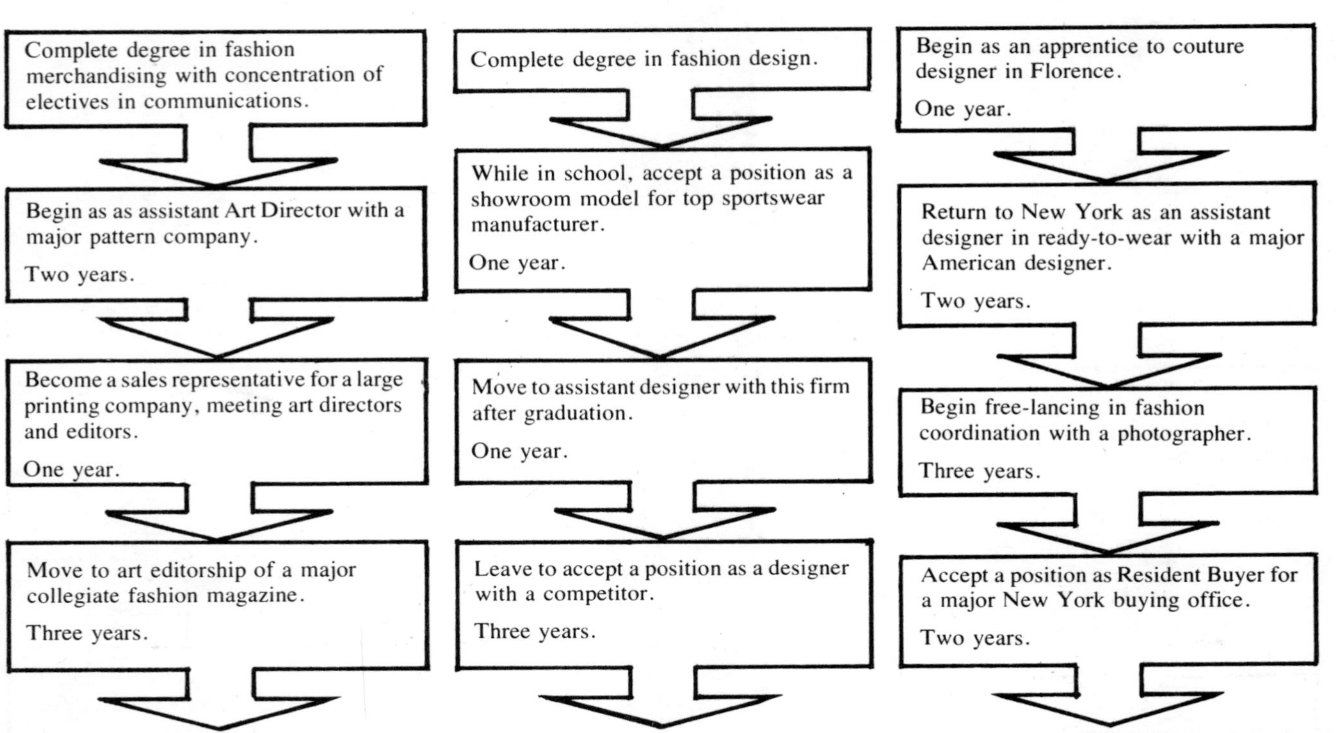

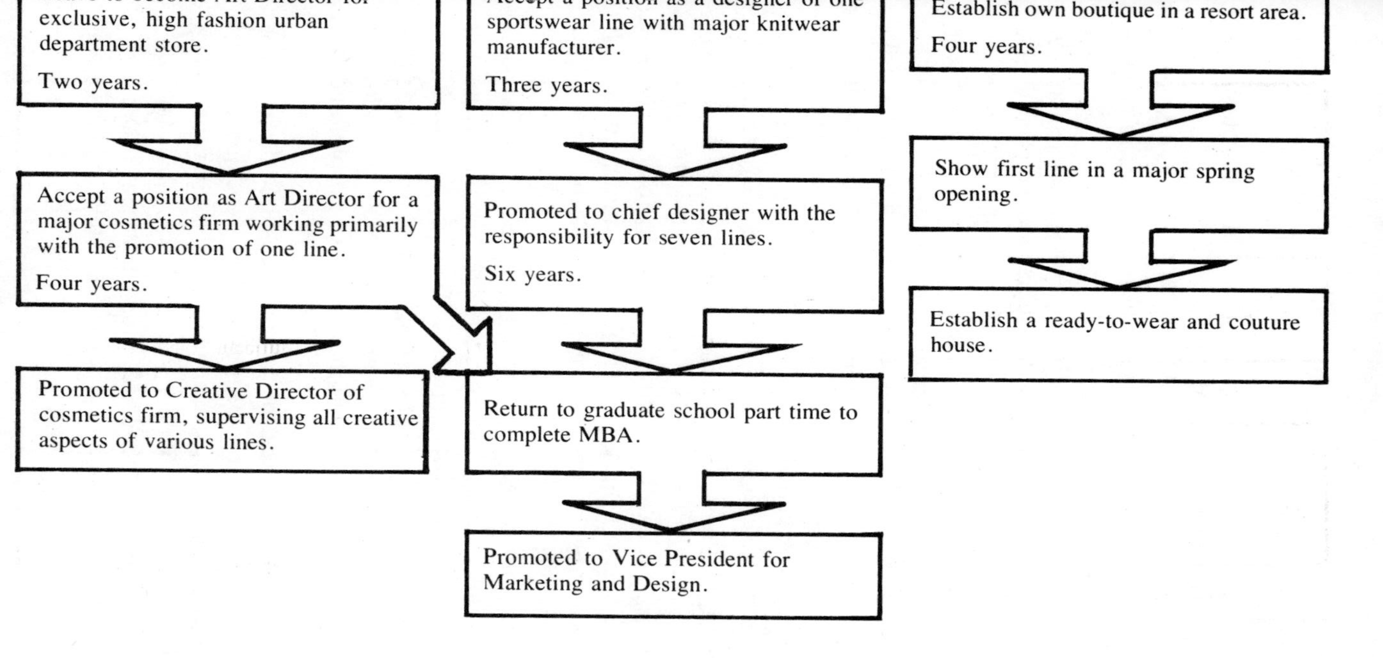
exclusive, high fashion urban department store.
Two years.
Accept a position as Art Director for a major cosmetics firm working primarily with the promotion of one line.
Four years.
Promoted to Creative Director of cosmetics firm, supervising all creative aspects of various lines.
sportswear line with major knitwear manufacturer.
Three years.
Promoted to chief designer with the responsibility for seven lines.
Six years.
Return to graduate school part time to complete MBA.
Promoted to Vice President for Marketing and Design.
Establish own boutique in a resort area.
Four years.
Show first line in a major spring opening.
Establish a ready-to-wear and couture house.

large city. A merchandising career can also be pursued—usually following a reasonable amount of retail buying experience—in many fashion related industries such as cosmetics, fiber, and fabrics, or with merchandising services in resident buying offices.

You might begin working in a boutique or specialty shop, and although this is considered more of a selling job, you can always consider opening your own business providing you have the capital and have learned the techniques of running a business—taxes, marketing, labor relations, profit, and loss. The Small Business Administration, an agency of the United States Government, is set up for the purpose of assisting people to get started in small businesses, and they are located in almost all cities. Along with knowledge of textiles, trends, and taxes, it is essential to be able to meet and deal with people because they are your raison d'être. You can hope to educate your customers, but if Ms. Five by Five wants circular stripes in plum and pink, you may be stuck with that dirndl. However, if you catch on, and are willing to work long hours, your business can flourish and the first thing you know you are hiring salespersons, seamstresses, and designers.

You may want to become a specialist in the design of apparel and work with children and teenagers who have handicaps and who need special kinds of garments. There are senior citizens who need the same kind of assistance and whose incomes are limited. Simple, inexpensive apparel with flair and color can make a world of difference to these kinds of people, and you have made a contribution.

You may want to teach, or become a costume designer, or branch out into home furnishings design. Teaching requires special courses, and if post-secondary schools are your preference, going on for the Master's degree is essential. Costume designing is easier to do in local community theater than in the Broadway theater, which requires special study and a special exam. To become a costume designer, you need a solid background in the history of costume and the history of theater so that you will know how to design for the cast of an eighteenth-century French farce or an avant garde Albee play. Home furnishings, fabrics, and a myriad of accessories from ceramics and pillows to tableware and furniture utilize many of the same talents of the creative fashion-conscious individual.

If you choose apparel design you need to keep up with the times, and be ahead of the seasons. Research in and use of fabric is mandatory; and deciding what people will buy is more than mere speculation, it is having a sixth sense, combined with a knowledge of good design, and hard work.

Refer to:
Chapter III: *Environmental Design*
Chapter VII: *Textile Design*
ChapterXI: *Theater Arts*

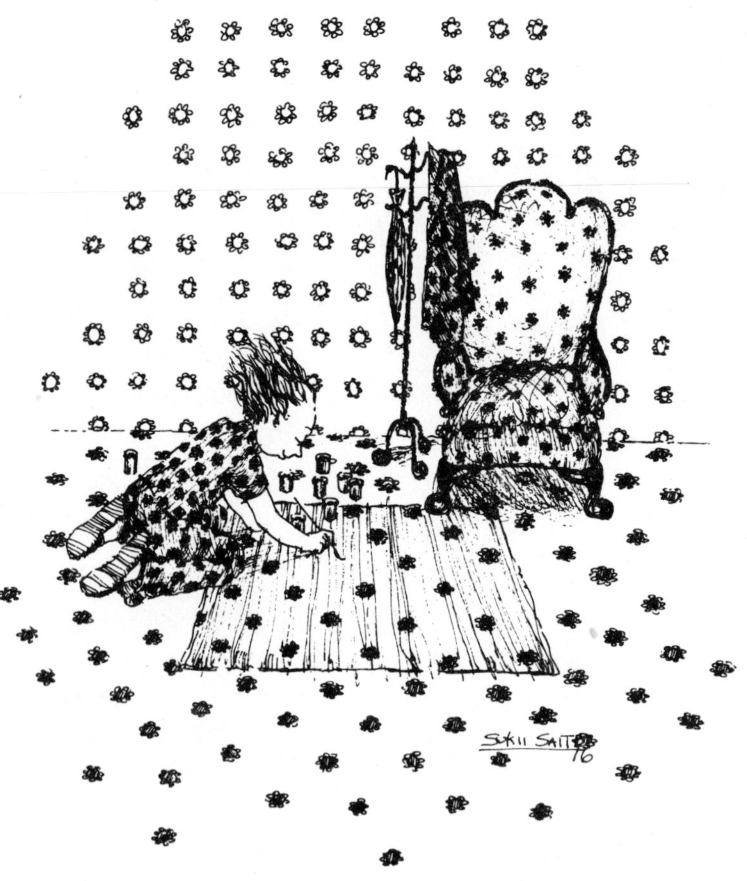

CHAPTER VII

Textile Design

You may choose the field of textile design because you are interested in painting and sculpture and want to apply these two- and three-dimensional design talents to a field where employment is available. As a textile designer you can work in print design, work with color on a flat surface, or work in woven design, taking fibers and constructing them to make a pattern. You will need to be conscious of the clothes people wear, the upholstery on furniture, the coverings on walls and floors, the curtains and draperies on windows, the linens on beds and tables, and the interiors of planes, trains, and automobiles. Wherever there is fabric, there has been a textile designer, and the design can be as simple as a man's shirt or as complicated as an exquisite wall hanging.

Education

Educationally, an art school or a college teaching textile design are preferred, especially one where you can get a foundation in color, drawing, and two- and three-dimensional design. You may elect courses in painting, printmaking, or ceramics; and you should have access to the apparel design department and the interior design department. Specific textile design course work may include use of hand looms/power looms; study of natural and synthetic fibers; design of knit patterns; effects of pattern, color, and texture; and history of textiles. Presentation techniques and a knowledge of photography will be helpful because you will need to take your own slides to show to clients, employers, or gallery directors.

After Graduation

You may want to work for a large manufacturer designing for the general public, for a small design house with exclusive designs, in a museum with a fabric collection, as a free-lancer selling your work, or in your own shop and taking individual orders. Some textile designers work for greeting card companies, designing wrapping paper and party goods; for wallpaper and linoleum companies; for home furnishing fabric manufacturers and showrooms; and for interior designers working with clients in the selection of fabrics. To begin, you will generally find the well-known large houses more inclined to hire recent graduates. The small exclusive design studios want experienced designers with established reputations. Free-lancing or setting up your own shop requires good experience with an opportunity for potential clients. This is usually achieved following several years of working for someone else. Some individuals become involved with textile engineering or textile chemistry and move into research, but these are special fields and require additional technical education.

After You Are Hired

On your first job you may be a colorist, checking the range and standards of color for fabrics; a fabric designer, creating print or woven materials; a design assistant, doing pattern repeats, layouts, coloring; or a stylist adapting motifs.

Provided business is good, advancement usually comes with experience, recognition of talents, and a willingnesss to work hard. The textile industry demands a person have, along with a creative mind, a head for business, energy, and ability to articulate well. Often a textile designer is an integral part of the sales effort of the organization.

The Years Ahead

The business may lead to many different kinds of jobs. You may be a head designer in the textile industry; a fashion coordinator in either the apparel or textile industry; a free-lancer who designs for the industry; an owner of a crafts shop creating and selling your own fabrics, designing textiles for a shop or series of shops; a curator of textiles in a museum; a textile historian; or a teacher in combination with any of the above textile jobs. If you lean towards textile design as a fine art, creating one-of-a-kind wall hangings (some of which may be three-dimensional) and floor coverings, you will begin to make contact with galleries and museums, as well as crafts fairs, and you will need a steady clientele to support you. Teaching can be especially valuable here.

Textile Design Career Paths

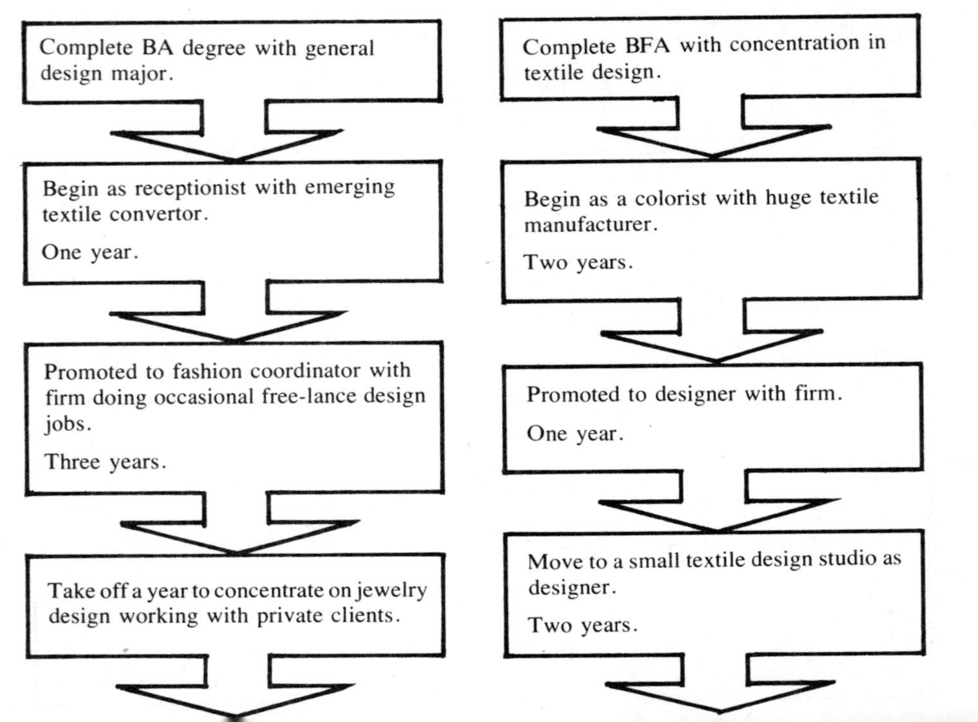

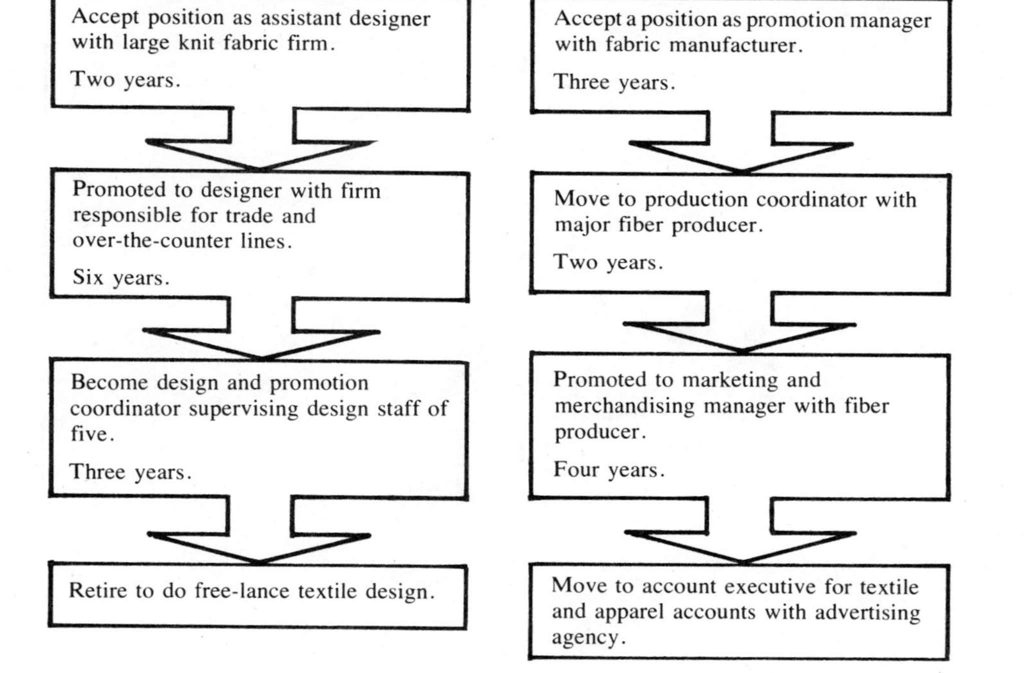
Accept position as assistant designer with large knit fabric firm.
Two years.
Promoted to designer with firm responsible for trade and over-the-counter lines.
Six years.
Become design and promotion coordinator supervising design staff of five.
Three years.
Retire to do free-lance textile design.
Accept a position as promotion manager with fabric manufacturer.
Three years.
Move to production coordinator with major fiber producer.
Two years.
Promoted to marketing and merchandising manager with fiber producer.
Four years.
Move to account executive for textile and apparel accounts with advertising agency.

agazine edit
art dire
Swiss
borderline
photostat
color
shoot concept
say hear
bleed
triangle
50%

CHAPTER VIII

Graphic Design

Graphic design is a visual language, a process by which the designer assembles shapes, color, and forms to create a message. As a graphic designer you deal not only with the image, but how the image should be transmitted, by what vehicle, and in what medium. Your responsibility is to inform and to make this information readily understandable by whoever is receiving it.

Graphic design embraces many areas of communication, but falls essentially into these categories: the design of books, magazines, brochures, packages, and the publications of business and industry; the multi-media field of computer graphics, audio-visual, film, slides, tapes; and the creation of images for posters, signs, books and magazine covers, photographic essays, advertisements, and symbols.

In all categories you will work with visual material, for your media are photographs, manuscripts, type faces, paper, printing processes, ink, paint, silk screen, and lettering. Because most publications, commercial printing of photographs, and written material are mass-produced, you will need to be aware of production and the conditions imposed by the various processes and manufacturing services. You will need to be visually sensitive and to be able to work with words and symbols, choosing that medium which is appropriate to your purpose. As a planning collaborator you will work closely with people from a variety of backgrounds and disciplines, and you must be able to work on a project from inception to implementation.

Education

Good academic training is essential and should include perspective drawing, lettering, design, color harmony, typography, composition, lithography, photography, layout, illustration technique, and, if possible, film and liberal arts subjects. Somewhere along the line business practices, marketing, report writing, and public speaking should be added as you advance in the progression. Because interpreting your ideas to people is paramount, it is important to be sensitive to people's feelings, to be articulate, and to be aware of the trends and changes, not only in your field, but in contemporary thought.

After Graduation

Your job search will include design departments of business and industrial firms, design consulting firms, publishing houses, TV stations, architectural firms (for architectural graphics and signage), advertising agencies (although this is more specialized), art departments of galleries, museums, and libraries, college and university publication offices, and freelancing (usually after gaining experience in the aforementioned). Your geographical location can be any of the fifty states and in both large and small enterprises.

After You Are Hired

Your first job may be very unglamorous as a layout artist or assistant designer doing paste-ups and mechanicals, lettering, fast sketches, photostats, and art work for the printer, but with talent and training in no time you can move on to creative designing and the challenging aspects of presenting your client's ideas to him graphically.

The Years Ahead

From the first job as a layout artist to creative director, owning your studio, or heading a consulting group, you will need to become recognized for the kind of work you do. Receiving awards, being asked to teach or speak or write about your particular design capabilities, assisting in a multi-media competition, and word of mouth are ways of achieving recognition. It comes with experience and the ability to create a design, to implement a plan, and to make a unique presentation.

As in any professional field, designers abound, but those who are moving ahead are those who are looking ahead with the capacity to see the relationship between the functional and the aesthetic aspects of design. When this combination is realized, you have made one of your first steps toward being your own designer. While this is happening to you, it is important to keep in mind the tensions that may develop with time deadlines, budget limitations, and the demands of employers. Although the competition is keen, the prospects are good, and the potential salary for those who achieve is rewarding.

Graphic Design Career Paths

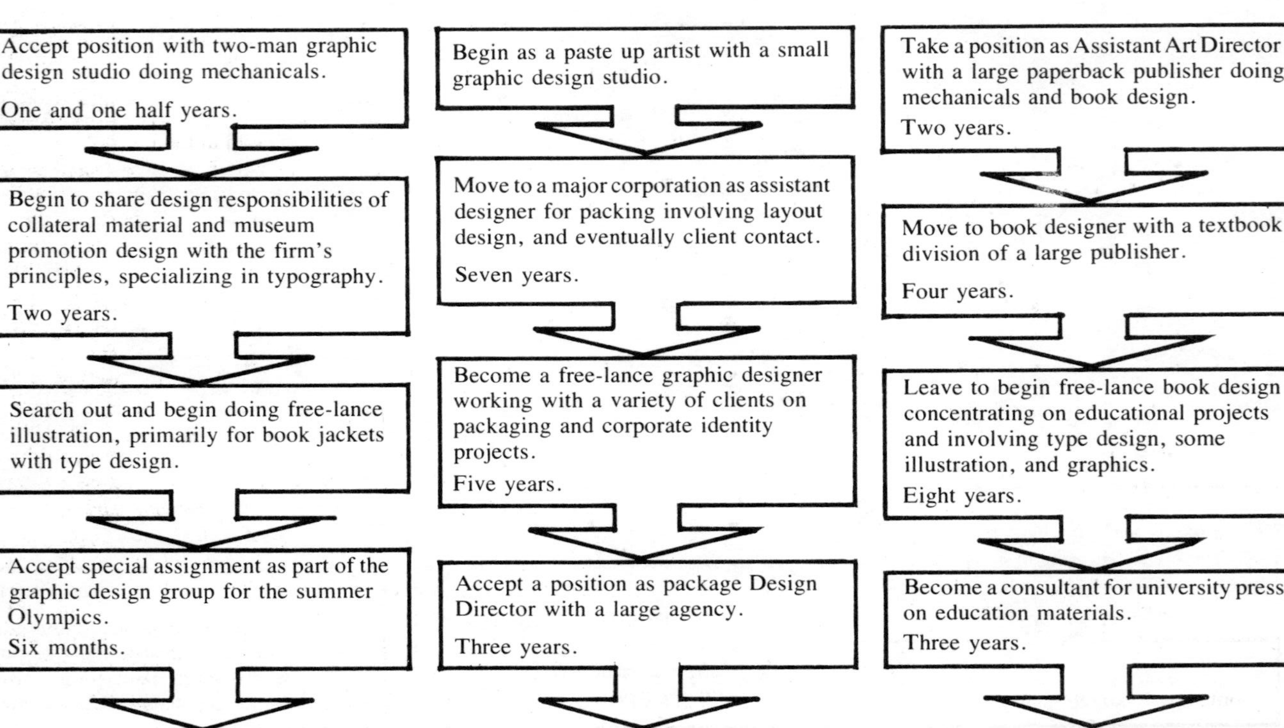

Return to free-lance staff position with large, well-known graphic design studio. Most projects concentrate on typography and illustration.

Three years.

Recent work featured as "up-and-coming" young graphic designer in professional magazine.

Move to advertising agency as Typography Director.

Eight years.

Continue to pursue free-lance illustration and design in the publishing world.

Move to Vice President, Graphic Design, with a large industrial design consulting firm concentrating on packaging and corporate identity programs.

Complete Master's degree in education.

One year.

Develop experimental educational materials on all aspects of design and production.

ArnieTen '76

CHAPTER IX

Advertising Design

Advertising is a business which helps sell products or services using the most appropriate media, whether it be newspapers, magazines, radio, or television, to reach the greatest number of potential buyers. Design for these media is concerned with the creation, planning, and execution of visual concepts through mass media. Here the concept is all important. The idea for an ad or ad campaign, when well conceived, is the basis for all the remaining visual design. Most advertising design is produced by advertising agencies, although some firms continue to use an "in-house" staff for a portion of their advertising programs.

Education

Your training in advertising will probably involve a specialized major, which will include communications design and art direction. In addition, you will want to become involved with the support media of your field: graphic design, illustration, photography, typography, two- and three-dimensional design, film, and video. Because it is critical that the advertising designer or art director be able to communicate effectively both verbally and visually, liberal arts should be an essential part of your education.

Advertising Career Paths

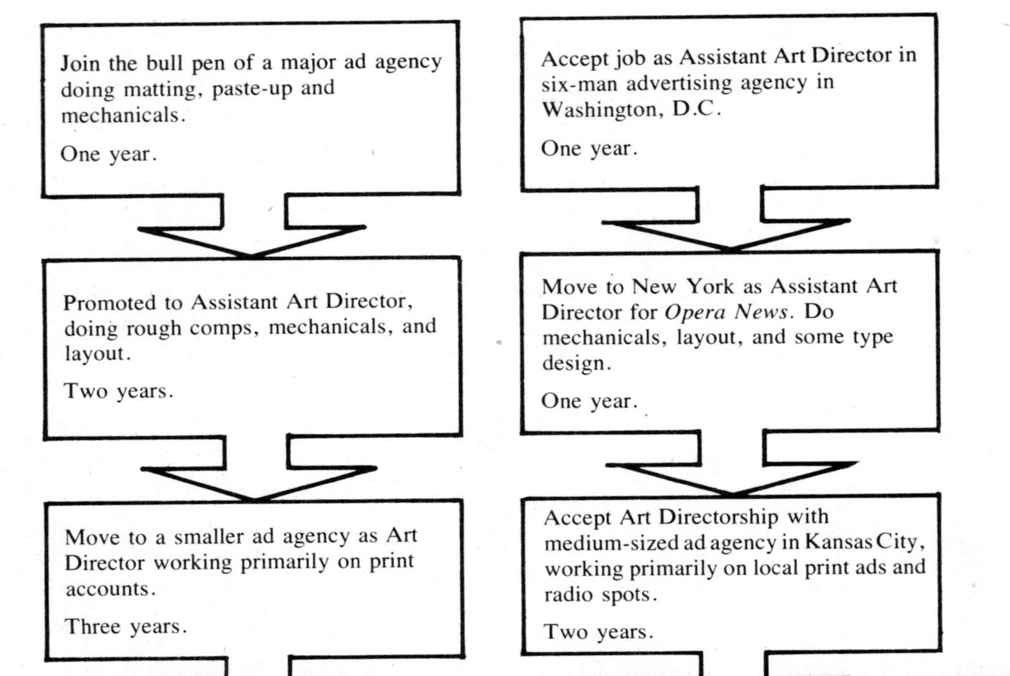

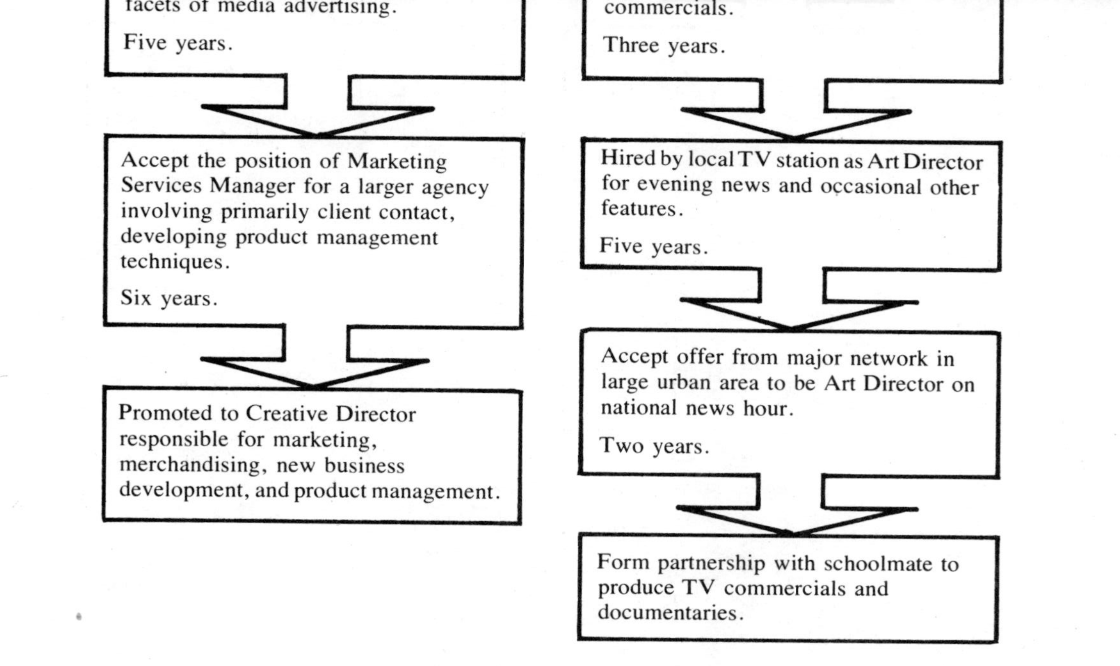
facets of media advertising.
Five years.
Accept the position of Marketing Services Manager for a larger agency involving primarily client contact, developing product management techniques.
Six years.
Promoted to Creative Director responsible for marketing, merchandising, new business development, and product management.
commercials.
Three years.
Hired by local TV station as Art Director for evening news and occasional other features.
Five years.
Accept offer from major network in large urban area to be Art Director on national news hour.
Two years.
Form partnership with schoolmate to produce TV commercials and documentaries.

After Graduation

If your goal is to work for an advertising agency, you will probably have to begin in the "bull pen," or as an assistant art director doing paste-ups, mechanicals, matting, letterings, and roughs. Although this is a less than glamorous position, it allows you to learn a tremendous amount of technical information and skills. Normally, you have been hired for your first position in an agency because of your potential for creating original advertising concepts, your craftsmanlike portfolio, and how you think on paper in presenting a visual concept. With this potential you can look forward to a promotion as an Art Director, which can happen in as little as three months or take as long as several years. Sometimes, it is necessary to change from one agency to another in order to be promoted.

After You Are Hired

Now you are an Art Director. You are responsible for conceiving advertising campaigns and "directing" the work of illustrators, photographers, graphic designers, layout artists, filmmakers, television producers, and type designers, who pool their talents and, with your execution, produce the end product which matches or even improves your original concept.

The Years Ahead

As an Art Director you may also seek work within the business and industrial world on a corporate advertising staff, in publishing, motion pictures, or television. Further advancement can include becoming Creative Director or moving laterally into marketing, management, or promotion planning.

The advertising world is one of the most exciting, most demanding, and constantly changing career experiences available to the artist or designer. It requires an agile and creative imagination perhaps even more than a refined artistic talent, combined with a high degree of energy to sell yourself and your ideas.

You should be aware, however, that in this unique, idea-oriented field, promotion often leads you away from creative art work towards management and administration.

CHAPTER X

Illustration

The professional illustrator uses pictorial means for mass communication in books, magazines, advertising, television, and film animation by providing a visual accompaniment for the printed word. The illustrator is often thought of as a painter whose pictures contribute greater clarity, impact, and directness to the writer's words.

Education

This combination of fine arts and illustration is more easily attained in art school, and the course work which leads to this training should include drawing, color, two- and three-dimensional design, anatomy, painting, silk screening, and graphic processes as well as the study of illustration techniques and concepts. Because an illustrator's work is seen in its reproduced form, training to prepare artwork for reproduction processes is considered essential.

As you progress in the profession, it is strongly suggested you add liberal arts to improve your communication skills; report writing to help you learn writing skills; marketing, promotion, and business procedures to assist you in your business relationships, since you are primarily a self-employed artist. As an artist you may want to continue with painting or add ceramics, sculpture, and printmaking to your list of accomplishments, and photography to enable you to take your own slides.

After Graduation

Beginning jobs are competitive and the less talented or mediocre usually find it difficult getting started. In any case you will pound pavements showing your portfolio. You will write letters to art directors. You will follow-up every lead from friends, faculty, newspapers, and professional journals. You will use your career planning office, you will leave or mail your portfolio or promotional material to art directors, and you will recontact those people who indicate an interest in your potential.

After You Are Hired

As an illustrator you may work for a publishing house doing book covers, spot illustrations for textbooks, or full-color children's books; for an advertising agency as a sketch artist visualizer and in preparing comprehensive layouts; for a magazine art department assisting the art director in planning the design of each issue; in a museum in exhibition and promotion design; in television in the preparation of slides and film animation; in theater as a set designer; in studios working with pictorial content; in greeting card companies designing cards, paper products, and books; in a fashion house sketching apparel; in U.S. Government publication offices; in medicine doing medical illustration (a highly technical kind of illustration for which additional education is needed); and in education preparing visual materials.

The Years Ahead

The years ahead may find you free-lancing for the book industry in full-color children's books, juveniles, textbooks, or fiction; as an editorial illustrator in a magazine; or in the apparel industry as a fashion illustrator. If you are an illustrator who free-lances for advertising agencies and in design studios, you will need other kinds of technical skills and a background in graphic design.

Once you have established a "track record" of reliability and ingenuity you can seek an artist's representative, whose job is to represent you to art directors, particularly in the advertising and publishing fields for which they will charge a percentage of your fee (usually 25 percent). In exchange for their percentage, they show your portfolio, take care of negotiations of price, royalties, and billing, and introduce you to new opportunities. It may be a representative who works with a group of illustrators (usually no more than 8 or 10), or it may be a new "rep" establishing himself/herself and eager to serve—often a good bet. A rep usually expects a full-time commitment from the illustrator. Turning down work may be justified, but if it persists, the artist may be dropped. Free-lancing is generally for the experienced illustrator familiar with the larger urban centers. Once established, however, geographic location is a matter of choice.

If you become an art director you may work for any of the aforementioned organizations plus large corporations whose art departments publish house organs, newspapers, brochures, and annual reports. Maybe you will become a teacher in combination with the above or a partner in a studio, which, of course, requires a knowledge of business procedures and practices. If you have three-dimensional interests and abilities, the path of exhibit designer in a gallery or museum is realistic.

As you can see, the career of the illustrator leads to many paths and because it can combine the fine artist with the designer, possibilities are endless. The most important aspect is that you recognize your strengths and pursue them accordingly.

Illustration Career Paths

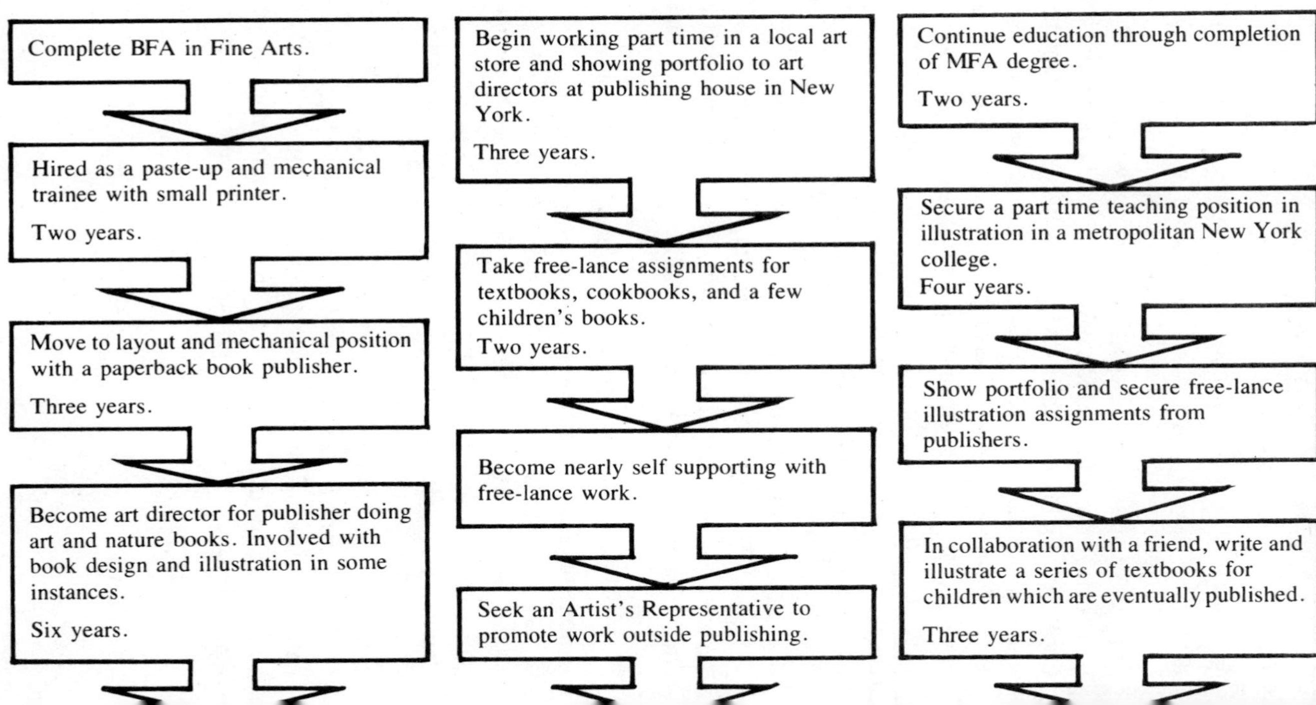

Begin showing illustration and design work to other publishers and receive free-lance assignments.

Ten years.

Establish own firm offering full service design and illustration to authors and publishers.

Devote full time to illustration with editorial and advertising assignments brought in by the rep.

Accept a full-time appointment at the Metropolitan Art School teaching illustration and graphic design.

Seven years.

Continue to consult with educational materials publishers on graphic and illustrative design.

CHAPTER XI

Theater Arts

The world of the theater offers several career choices including scenic, costume, and lighting design. These three "theater arts" are integral requirements for the production of most theatrical events including Broadway musicals, repertory theater, opera, summer stock, dinner theater, community theater productions, films, television, TV commercials, and even the circus. The scenic designer creates the scenes with one or more stage sets; the lighting designer creates the atmosphere on the stage; and the costume designer designs and produces the actors' garments whether they be contemporary or period dress.

Education

A basic training in art and design is essential for the theater artist, including foundation design courses, painting, sculpture, light, and color. More specialized courses in scenic design and painting, lighting design, costume design, theatrical design history, interior design, and fashion design and construction are essential to theatrical designers no matter which area they ultimately choose as their specialization. You may seek out a particular curriculum which offers theater arts concentrations on the Bachelor's level or you may choose to continue your studies on the graduate level leading to a Master's degree. The educational institutions offering these programs may be found

Theater Arts Career Paths

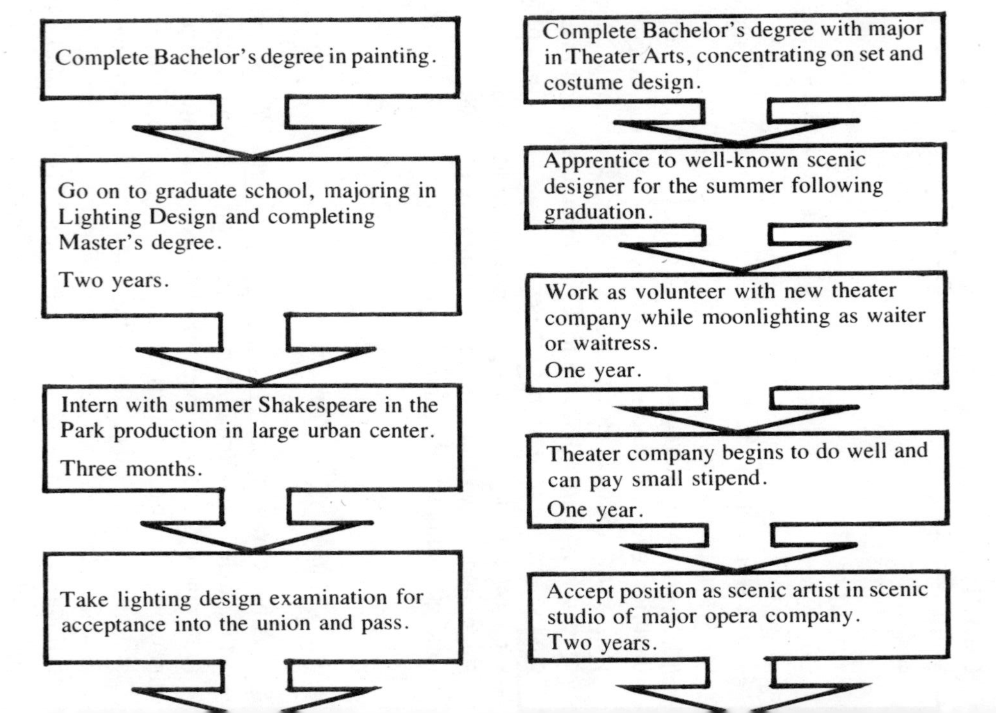

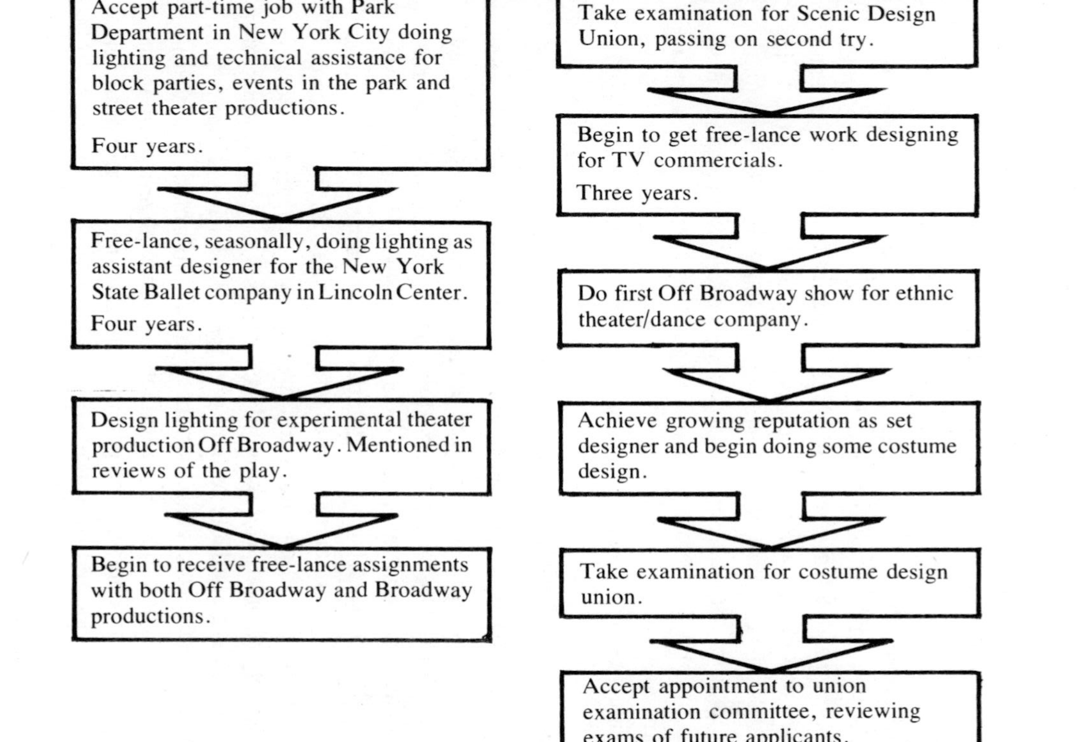
Accept part-time job with Park Department in New York City doing lighting and technical assistance for block parties, events in the park and street theater productions.
Four years.
Free-lance, seasonally, doing lighting as assistant designer for the New York State Ballet company in Lincoln Center.
Four years.
Design lighting for experimental theater production Off Broadway. Mentioned in reviews of the play.
Begin to receive free-lance assignments with both Off Broadway and Broadway productions.
Take examination for Scenic Design Union, passing on second try.
Begin to get free-lance work designing for TV commercials.
Three years.
Do first Off Broadway show for ethnic theater/dance company.
Achieve growing reputation as set designer and begin doing some costume design.
Take examination for costume design union.
Accept appointment to union examination committee, reviewing exams of future applicants.

by writing to the American Theater Society, Inc., 226 West 47th, New York, New York 10036.

After Graduation

Although this is an exciting and glamorous field, it generally offers sporadic employment. Theater people may work one show and then wait some time before another opportunity becomes available. Almost all the creative areas of the theater are unionized, which further restricts easy entry into the field for the beginner. Your best starting place is summer stock, repertory, or small theater companies away from major cities, some of which may not be unionized. You may have to work as an apprentice (without salary) in the beginning, but this is valuable experience and will help you attain your ultimate goal.

After You Are Hired

Admission to the unions is by examination and in some industries, such as portions of the motion picture business, may be followed by an apprenticeship period where a lower pay rate is earned. However, once you are a full-fledged member of the union, some of the disadvantages of intermittent employment are offset by union pay scales which are fairly high. The examinations for union admission are highly competitive and extremely thorough, taking place over several days. Special courses are available to help prepare the aspiring designer for these specialized examinations. Further information concerning the scheduling of examinations, specialized training or preparatory courses, and potential earning of a theater designer can be requested from the nearest union local, such as

United Scenic Artists
1540 Broadway
New York, N.Y. 10023

The Years Ahead

Since the majority of work in theater design, particularly that related to either the motion picture or television industries, takes place on the west coast center of Hollywood or the east coast center of New York, a career in theater design may have geographic restrictions if you set your sights high. However, you can often find equally satisfying and perhaps even more frequent work with a local repertory theater company, university theater group, opera company, and the like. Those who do pursue this kind of theater experience may work in any number of careers and have the dual satisfaction of a vocation and an avocation. Many a community theater looks towards its citizens for support and active participation.

The bright lights of Broadway and the challenge of Hollywood offer a tempting dream but a career path with this as an ultimate goal requires careful consideration and constant reassessment combined with a little bit of luck and a lot of drive.

CHAPTER XII

Fine Arts

Fine arts are usually thought of as painting, printmaking, and sculpture; actually it includes glass blowing, photography, wall hangings (textiles), drawing, ceramics, wood carving, and metalsmithing if these pieces are created as ends in themselves. They are the result of the artist's creativity based on education and imagination. To decide on and pursue this kind of career takes drive and talent and is the realistic goal of very few. But for those few it is worth every minute of the demands that the life style will make, and no other life style will seem acceptable.

You begin preparing for your career early on—maybe with the first paint box or silly putty or wood work; but you begin to be serious when you take your art classes seriously and realize that, as important as other courses are, the highlight of your class work is that canvas or model or pot or piece of wood you can work on uninterruptedly. You will begin to work at home and ask for a place in your house to set up a small studio. You may take Saturday morning or after-school art classes. Going to museum shows becomes as important as going to picture shows. You are goal directed.

Education

Your next choice is the selection of an art school, college, or university with an art department that offers an art major. You now begin a rarified experience.

Because it is important to have a well-rounded education,

you will take life drawing, two- and three-dimensional design, lettering, color, perspective drawing, photography, art history, and liberal arts. Artists today more than ever need to be able to use words and to communicate with each other, with their patrons, and with their galleries. While in school, you will be wise to become competent in the skills of your profession, whether they be making frames, framing pictures, stretching canvases, constructing a kiln, welding, making a loom, packing your work, and hanging a show. You will, of course, learn to take and develop your own slides, because it is expensive to hire a photographer, and a slide becomes one of the most important things in life for the fine artist. It is through slides that you may get a job, enter a contest, be admitted to a gallery, win a grant, or be accepted into graduate school. Your slides are your portfolio. Original works of art are too precious and too cumbersome to send through the mail or carry from place to place with you.

After Graduation

You have learned many of these things, and you graduate with your Bachelor's degree. Now what? Do you get a job in a greeting card company; do you sell reproductions at the sales desk in a museum; do you act as receptionist in a gallery; do you become a colorist in a textile factory; do you take courses to prepare for teaching—education courses for public school, the MFA for post-secondary teaching; do you "go commercial"; or do you take any job, such as waiting on table, driving a cab, doing carpentry, selling shoes? What you probably will not do is enter a non-art related business or industry if you represent 30 percent of the people who are dedicated to becoming fine artists.

You may want to consider your own "biological time clock"

and take a hard look at how and when you work during a normal day. If you are truly committed to being a fine artist, your peak periods of productivity should be reserved for doing your own work. Your job may then need to be one offering atypical hours.

However you may work in any of the aforementioned, and if you really are motivated, you will find time each week, each month, each year to work in your studio, to enter shows, and to accept commissions which, if you become really well known may, at some future time, be your means of livelihood. This takes many years and a wealth of experience. It is worth mentioning that most fine artists become bored with menial jobs, and when this happens they usually look for a career in teaching because it allows them more time to work.

"*Fine artists*—painters, sculptors, printmakers, and ceramists—go into teaching, usually after getting a Master of Fine Arts degree and looking for a post-secondary position. A goodly number remain in their studios—often assisted by grants from foundations, Government, and a few patrons—painters (25 percent), sculptors (35 percent), and ceramists (50 percent) (more people buy pots than paintings). Some enter communication design in the media and publishing fields, but the largest number to leave fine arts are the painters (15 percent) who go into non-profit fields such as social work, museum work, government work, and the like."[1]

It should be noted that formalized classroom teaching, although an ideal alternative for the fine artist, is a competitive field. It may become necessary to set up your own classes, teach at community centers, senior citizen centers, adult education centers, continuing education centers, in national or state government programs, or in library and museum programs. If as a

[1]Carolyn L. Hawes, "Artists Work at Art," *Journal of College Placement,* Summer, 1975, pp. 24, 70.

Fine Arts Career Paths

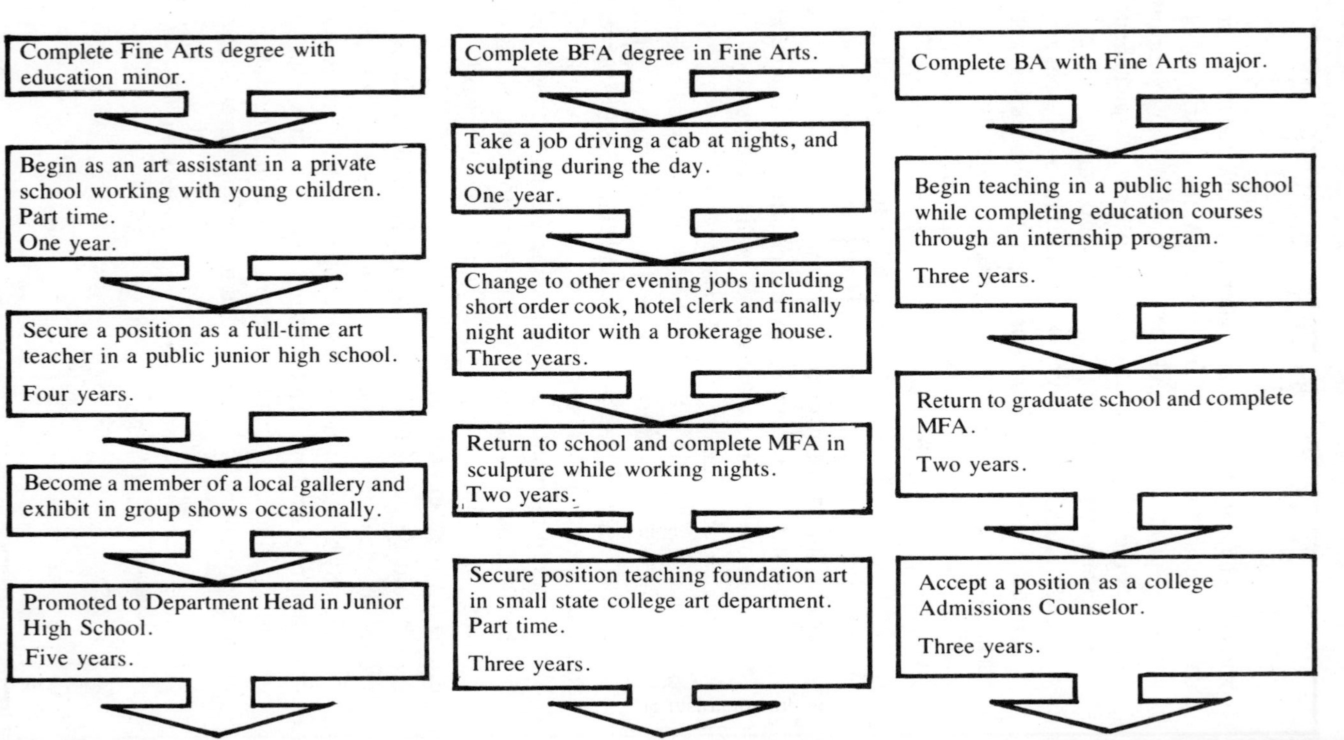

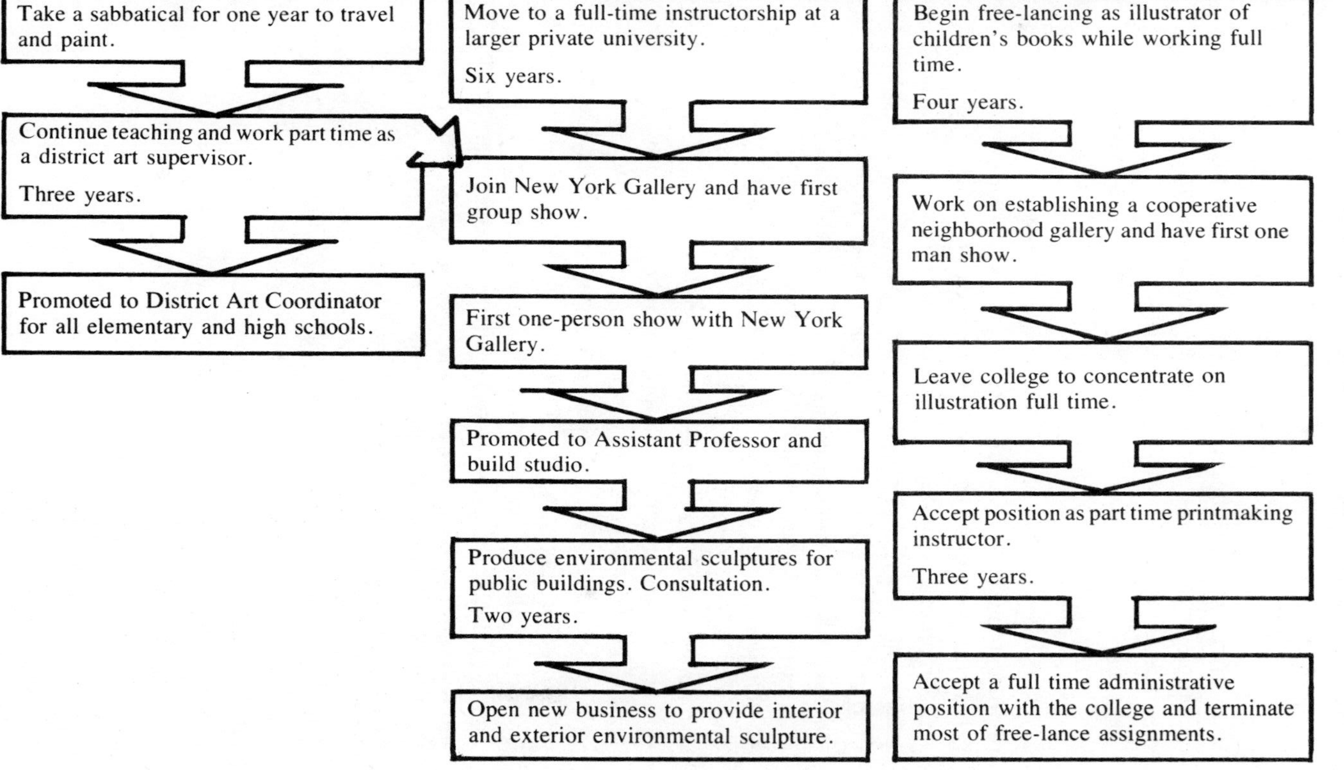
Take a sabbatical for one year to travel and paint.
Continue teaching and work part time as a district art supervisor.
Three years.
Promoted to District Art Coordinator for all elementary and high schools.
Move to a full-time instructorship at a larger private university.
Six years.
Join New York Gallery and have first group show.
First one-person show with New York Gallery.
Promoted to Assistant Professor and build studio.
Produce environmental sculptures for public buildings. Consultation.
Two years.
Open new business to provide interior and exterior environmental sculpture.
Begin free-lancing as illustrator of children's books while working full time.
Four years.
Work on establishing a cooperative neighborhood gallery and have first one man show.
Leave college to concentrate on illustration full time.
Accept position as part time printmaking instructor.
Three years.
Accept a full time administrative position with the college and terminate most of free-lance assignments.

fine artist, you go commercial, you will have to learn the techniques of that profession which can mean day, night, or special courses at one of the local art schools.

The Years Ahead

All artists want to exhibit, and getting into a gallery can be important, but pursuing the gallery scene too soon is not wise. It is better to get some experience in local exhibits, develop your skills, mature in your technique, and season your work. Make your name slowly and establish your reputation firmly. When you are ready, take your resume and your slides to those galleries whose concern for the artist is solid, after calling and requesting an appointment. If the gallery accepts you, you may be included first in group shows and ultimately have your own one-man or one-woman show. You will decide on your prices and remember the gallery gets anywhere from 40 percent to 60 percent of the sale price as well as charging for incurred expenses, such as advertising for a "one-man" show. So if you sell $5000 worth of work, your return is only about $2000 to $3000, before taxes, which is fine if it supplements an income or brings additional commissions, but it is not enough to live on in and of itself. Also, there are very few artists who are prodigious enough to have more than one show a year, and it is more likely that they will have a show about every two or three years. Getting a show together is a monumental task.

Lastly, there will be those fine artists whose interest in the arts will become an avocation. For those who choose other careers, this avocation will afford many satisfying hours and allow them to be active in local shows, fairs, and small neighborhood galleries without moving into the major market place.

CHAPTER XIII

Film

Filmmakers, like photographers, are generally oriented to personal commitment, social documentary, or the commercial world, with two major differences. One, filmmaking is a more expensive medium and often difficult to use creatively; and two, the film industry is unionized, which poses a problem of entry for the young aspirant. However, if you think your creativity lies in artistic creation by use of this highly technical medium, a more exciting pursuit is hard to find.

Education

There are only a few schools that offer film as a major, and it is important to look carefully for the one that will fit your needs. In the early days filmmakers learned by doing, and it is only recently that they have sought formal education.

To have a well-rounded education in film, you will want to include video, animation and production, cinematography, graphic design, and photography, along with foundation design courses and liberal arts courses to help you express yourself visually and verbally in this fascinating world. There are those who feel fine arts is a tremendous aid in filmmaking, and to know about make-up and history of costume and drama are pluses indeed. Many filmmakers began in other fields and moved into film as the medium became better known.

Attending film festivals and watching old films shown at

local theaters and museums are a must. Film is a new enough medium so that many famous directors are still living and available for seminars.

After Graduation

Your goal is to get a job, which might be accomplished directly via the union (highly selective) or through the side door via TV commercials and non-union small film companies. The fields which use and make films include industry and business, government, education, and the arts. The kinds of films may range from animation, feature films, industrial sales and training films, cartoons, shorts, commercials, to title graphics and even computer-generated graphics, a new field requiring a knowledge of film aesthetics and computer programming.

After You Are Hired

If you are lucky you might begin as an apprentice editor or assistant film editor, keeping track of exposed film, cataloging film, recording the editing process, sweeping the cutting room floor, and answering the telephone; as a production assistant manning the telephone, getting props, keeping notes, showing initiative in carrying out ideas; as an assistant director, coordinating the shooting, scouting locations, planning daily shooting schedules, calling extras and actors; as sound man responsible for all recorded sound during the production, for slating and identification for editing, for use and placement of microphones, for sound effects and their proper timing; as camera operator responsible to the director for what the camera records and how the camera functions.

The Years Ahead

When your training has been established, you can look forward to becoming a film director, which requires a background

Film Career Paths

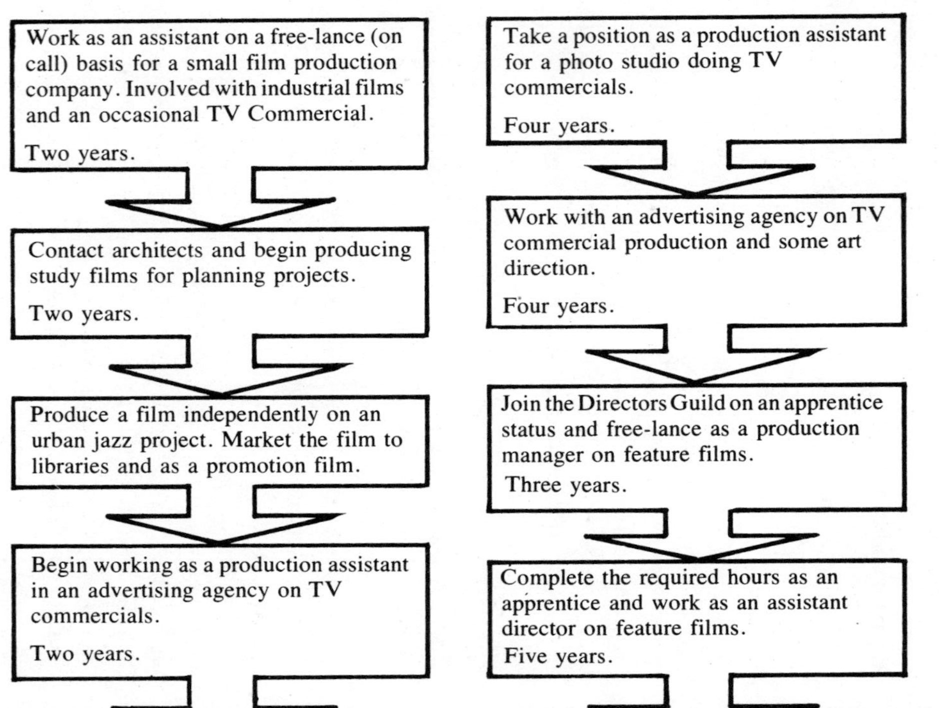

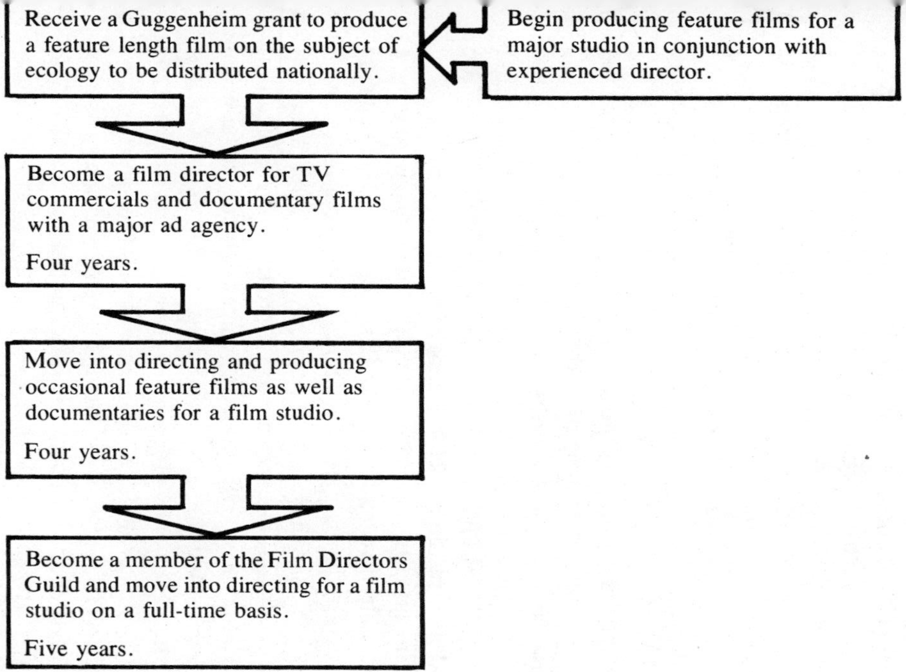

Begin producing feature films for a major studio in conjunction with experienced director.

Receive a Guggenheim grant to produce a feature length film on the subject of ecology to be distributed nationally.

Become a film director for TV commercials and documentary films with a major ad agency.

Four years.

Move into directing and producing occasional feature films as well as documentaries for a film studio.

Four years.

Become a member of the Film Directors Guild and move into directing for a film studio on a full-time basis.

Five years.

in film; a knowledge of video; a feeling for writing, music, and design; and a sensitivity to people. You achieve this by coming up through the ranks of film, TV, or advertising.

Most films, particularly those produced by motion picture studios, involve the talents of many others besides the director. There is the director of cinematography, a job often achieved by way of the camera with a background in film, writing, and acting. Then there is the producer, the major decision-maker of any film, who hires the director and crew; accepts scripts, sets, and costumes; and authorizes the budgets. Sometimes he directs, but mainly he is the executive for the film, often seeking financial support.

Other specialists include the art director, responsible for the composition and visual design of the film, including location, color and set decoration; the set decorator, who is involved in selecting and designing all the environments used in the film; the editor, who ultimately establishes the continuity and pacing of the film from the director's concepts.

As a fine arts filmmaker, you would be involved in making a film for your own satisfaction. This costly and continuous involvement requires getting a grant or being commissioned, neither of which is easy, but sometimes possible after other film successes. When film is pursued as a strictly creative medium, it requires the same dedication and career choices that concern the fine artist. One alternative available to filmmakers, whether they be pursuing a commercial or fine arts involvement, is teaching, which provides a stable income while a career is in its more formative stages. It is, however, somewhat of a paradox that like all teaching in specialized disciplines, you usually must have fairly substantial experience and training to secure a position in the increasingly competitive field of education.

Film is a field that is becoming increasingly important for educational purposes, industrial meetings and training sessions, and government archives. Feature-length films require the input of many specialists, each working on one aspect of the film. However, your future is bright if you have the drive and willingness to pursue a career that is both technical and aesthetic and makes no promises.

CHAPTER XIV

Video

Video is the baby of the media, and since equipment is expensive, its creative use is restricted to a limited number of artists who are still involved in developing the electronic visual-aural image. In this field, you will work with synthesizers and computer graphics; you will create commercials, station logos, and personal tapes; you will use it interchangeably with film for different effects; and you will be involved with research. Because this is such a new field, a great deal of experimentation is in order.

Since technology in this medium is still in its infancy, equipment is not standardized and consequently broad usage has only just begun. At present, video is largely used as a tool where immediacy is paramount and permanence is secondary. Many films and TV producers use video much like the photographer uses the Polaroid to check lighting, composition, and pacing before committing several retakes on film.

Video is also becoming a tool for educators and counselors because of the immediate feedback potential, relative low cost of tape which can be reused, and convenience of equipment. Social and community action agencies such as drug rehabilitation programs, community planning groups, or consumer advocacy programs often use video both as a feedback mechanism in counseling programs and as a promotion device to reach the public.

Training in video requires a visual education similar to that of the filmmaker with the added technical knowledge of the unique uses of the medium. Such training can be undertaken as part of a film curriculum or in conjunction with video workshops often available in most urban areas. The most critical aspect of training in video is access to equipment, which is an expensive initial investment.

Today, there are several types of experiences potentially available for participation in the production of video tapes as an intrinsic medium rather than as a support tool. Many major industries have established well-equipped video studios with the long-range goal of producing training tapes, computerized art work, and promotional or sales material. Television studios, particularly the Public Broadcasting Stations, have begun serious experimentation in creative uses of the video medium, although involvement here is often restricted to the established artist and television engineer. Several independent, creative video groups have sought and received foundation and arts council grants to explore video, to further training, and to produce creative work. A smaller number of specialized firms employing video as a tool for the production of work such as computer graphics have developed in recent years.

Video, because it is a new field, is truly a career with much to be discovered and invented. If you possess a pioneering spirit, involvement in this emerging field can challenge your enterprising abilities. Video truly is the wave of the future.

CHAPTER XV

Photography

As a photographer you are an artist who creates an image by use of a mechanical instrument, the camera, which may be very simple or quite complicated, inexpensive or costly, with a variety of attachments requiring sophistication and intense study. Your medium is film, either black and white or color. You can work in a large or small city, for a creative or non-creative employer, in a free-lance or staff position. However, every artist, architect, or designer should have at least one year of photography to learn how to take his own slides and to become aware of this artistic tool.

Education

From your high school you will probably go to an art school, an art college, or a technical institute to pursue a certificate or a degree. Occasionally a person becomes a professional photographer by taking pictures on his own and learning the techniques of the camera, but this is rare and generally not an easy way to success in the field. Your education is both visual and technical, and you should be aware that proficiency in technical skill is equally important to the development of your visual talents.

While a student you will make visits to galleries, museums, and studios to look at photographs and learn about photographers. You will attend openings of photographic exhibits and read professional journals.

After Graduation

The first job a photographer can get is the best one to take. It is a competitive field, and there always seem to be more candidates than jobs. The field is diversified, however, and ranges from the clearly technical to the purely fine arts. In between lie industrial photography, fashion photography, portrait photography, studio and advertising photography, magazine photography, news media photography, architectural photography, and even underwater photography. You can work in publishing, advertising, architecture, for greeting card companies, architectural firms, TV, education, the U.S. Government, business, industry, the theater, or as a medical photographer.

After You Are Hired

Most commercial photographers begin their careers as studio assistants, a job low in pay (and esteem) but high in experience. They do everything from sweeping floors to helping in the darkroom, and learn the myriad of technical necessities. There can be the added advantage of access to studio equipment after hours when you have been with a photographer for a reasonable period of time.

In advertising, you do the publication layouts, hire the models, help create the sets, work with the creative director, and meet the deadlines. In industry and business, beside providing photographs for all kinds of publications, from in-house newsletters to annual reports, you also photograph anything from mechanical complexities to slides for sales meetings.

In the Federal Government, you can work in many of the departments and you can photograph in the air or underwater. Mostly, of course, you will be on the ground, doing the same as any commercial photographer. There is an announcement made of these kinds of openings and you must apply directly. Announcements are found in post offices and other government

Photography Career Paths

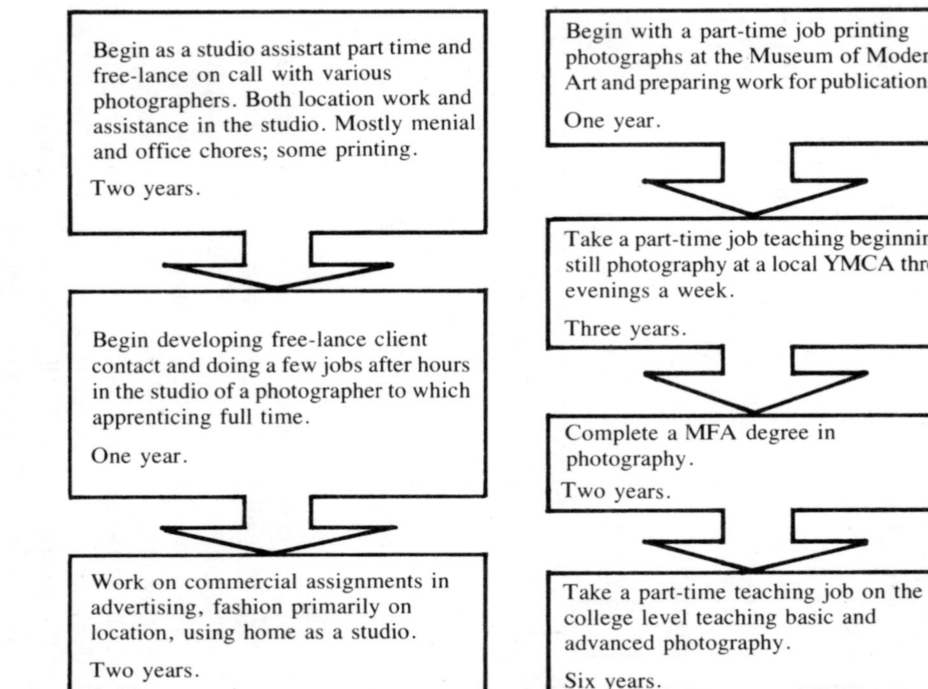

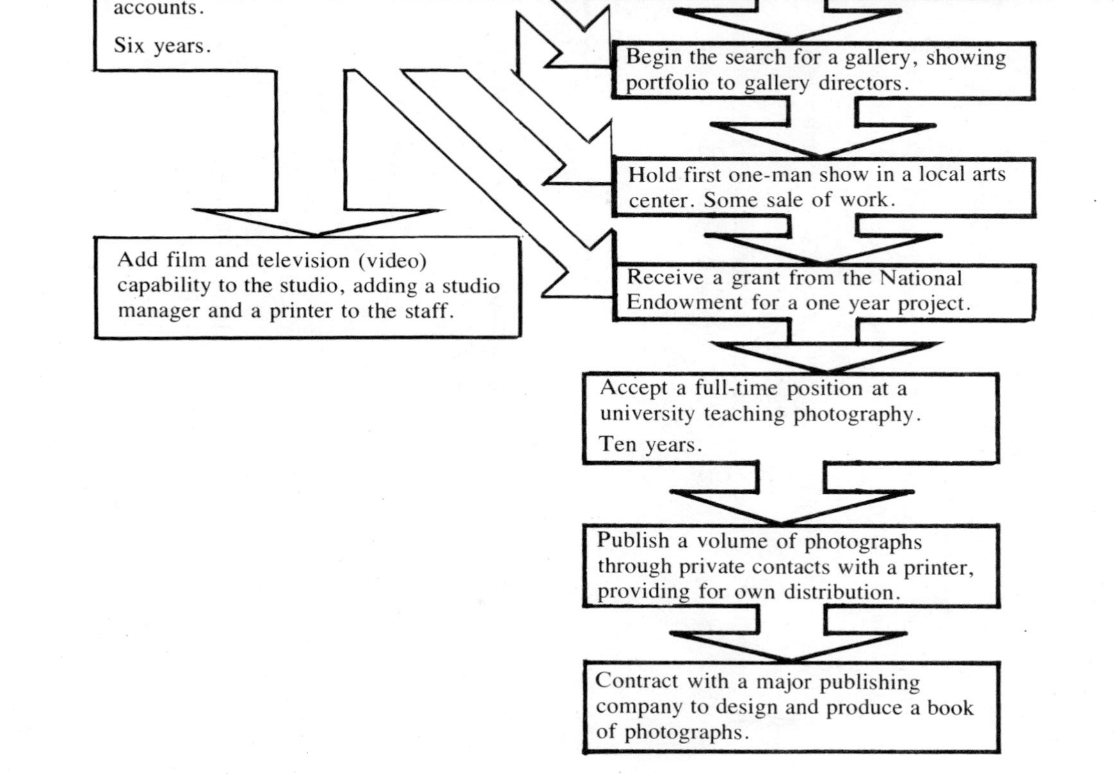
accounts.
Six years.
Add film and television (video) capability to the studio, adding a studio manager and a printer to the staff.
Begin the search for a gallery, showing portfolio to gallery directors.
Hold first one-man show in a local arts center. Some sale of work.
Receive a grant from the National Endowment for a one year project.
Accept a full-time position at a university teaching photography.
Ten years.
Publish a volume of photographs through private contacts with a printer, providing for own distribution.
Contract with a major publishing company to design and produce a book of photographs.

buildings as well as college career planning offices. No examination is required and the availability of equipment is excellent. Travel is sometimes involved, too.

In greeting card companies you provide photographs for books, brochures, games, and cards; in publishing for similar material as well as texts, manuals, and book jackets.

In TV, newspapers, and magazines you provide a story or a picture essay to support a story. You may be a staff photographer or a free-lance photographer, and you may have to sell your picture to justify the reason for taking it. Once you become good at this, you are sought after for regular features. Exciting, yes; competitive, again yes; but once you achieve a name, you can hire an artist's representative who will make contacts for you and let you choose your subjects.

The Years Ahead

If you become a free-lance photographer, you may work for publishing companies, newspapers, magazines, or house organs; for news media, such as TV, film, and newspapers; with advertising agencies and design studios; or in the fashion industry.

This is a career commitment which requires energy, dedication, and patience and enough clients who will continue to use your talents so that you can ultimately earn your own living.

Staff photographers work in the fields mentioned above as well as in museums, galleries, educational institutions, and medical facilities. However, staff jobs are difficult to find and generally offer less variety and potential for individual growth. As an alternative, you may wish to consider teaching in an art school, working in a community program, or teaching private students.

Many photographers choose to pursue this medium as a fine

art and earn their living either "commercially," while experimenting with the camera and keeping their aesthetic values, or in teaching. Galleries now have begun to specialize in photographic work and these shows are well attended and appreciated. Museums have collections of well-known photographers and viewing their work can be as exciting as viewing any other artistic medium.

ART
EDUCATION
#1

CHAPTER XVI

Art Education

As an art teacher you will begin to develop the creative abilities of your students by using your education and your knowledge of art. You will learn about the development of children and their differences in learning capacities and individual personalities.

A good art teaching program should cover the above areas as well as prepare teachers who will guide future generations of artists, designers, and educators.

The teaching field is a popular choice for the artist and in many ways one of the most rewarding. Because art teachers are artists, they should have the ability and interest to use their knowledge to encourage creativity and talent in those who aspire to become artists.

An art teaching career should begin with your asking yourself why you are choosing this career. You should know that it is a competitive field. You should know the rewards are high, but the rate of survival depends on your qualifications and your talent. You should know that the art teacher must work hard at continuing to be an artist as well as a teacher. You should not choose to be a teacher if you do not like people and children. A good teacher is able to communicate effectively and with understanding and at the same time act as a critic helping students progress by evaluating their work.

With a degree in Art Education, you may wonder if your job opportunities will be only in the public school systems. Because this is an area where the competition is the keenest, you need to be aware that there are teaching opportunities available in several other areas. In preparing art teachers for a world with uncertain employment availability, most teacher training colleges have become involved with educational programs other than those which apply to the public and private school systems. A few of these available options are: hospitals, community centers, museums, youth centers, educational television, government programs, toy manufacturers, and adult education.

Part of a program in teacher training might be directed toward any of these alternatives in the form of fieldwork, community interests, or outreach programs. The encouragement of visual and artistic expression is needed in the programs in day care centers, prisons, and in the teaching of the elderly and the exceptional child. During your college program as a student, you should explore these fields and become aware of the contribution that art education can make to other people's lives.

If you decide to become an art teacher, you should write for a list of schools which have art education programs leading to State Certification. A good source for this information is:

National Art Education Association
1916 Association Avenue
Reston, Virginia 22091

National Association of Schools of Art
1 Dupont Circle N.W.
Washington, D.C. 20036

An additional source of information for volunteer programs such as Action—a combination of Vista and the Peace Corps—and for suggestions of other Art Programs is: *New Roles for Educators*, a book published by the Harvard Graduate School of Education, written by Rita Weathersby, Patricia

Allen, and Allen Blackmer, Jr. It is highly informative and can probably be found in your school library.

Educationally and professionally it is an asset to choose an Art Education program offered in an Art School because of the ease and opportunity to familiarize yourself with the multiple areas of art and design.

Your studies should include design, crafts, film, photography, theater, art history, and the traditional courses of painting, drawing, sculpture, and printmaking.

Today's art teacher should also learn to use such instructional methods as video tape, slides, films, film strips, tape cassettes. You may want to learn to produce video tape and slide presentations. In your teaching program you will manage your own supplies and prepare your own lesson plans and materials. Since the educator must be able to communicate effectively in words, your program of study should include classes in English grammar, creative writing, educational psychology, and interpersonal relations.

An art education program will also include student teaching assignments, usually in the senior year. You will be assigned to a school where your work with a class will be done under a supervising teacher. These student teaching assignments may be in any chosen area of the country that has a student teaching program structured with your college.

The evaluation of your performance as a student teacher will constitute one of the most valuable factors in your finding a good position after graduation, and in some cases, if a vacancy occurs, the school where you did your student teaching will hire you.

Because of the competition among the graduates in art education programs, you will need to be knowledgeable about the preparation of a resume and skilled in the presentation of a good portfolio. If you have not consulted your college career planning office before your senior year, you should visit it early in that year. You will be offered assistance in the preparation of

Art Education Career Path

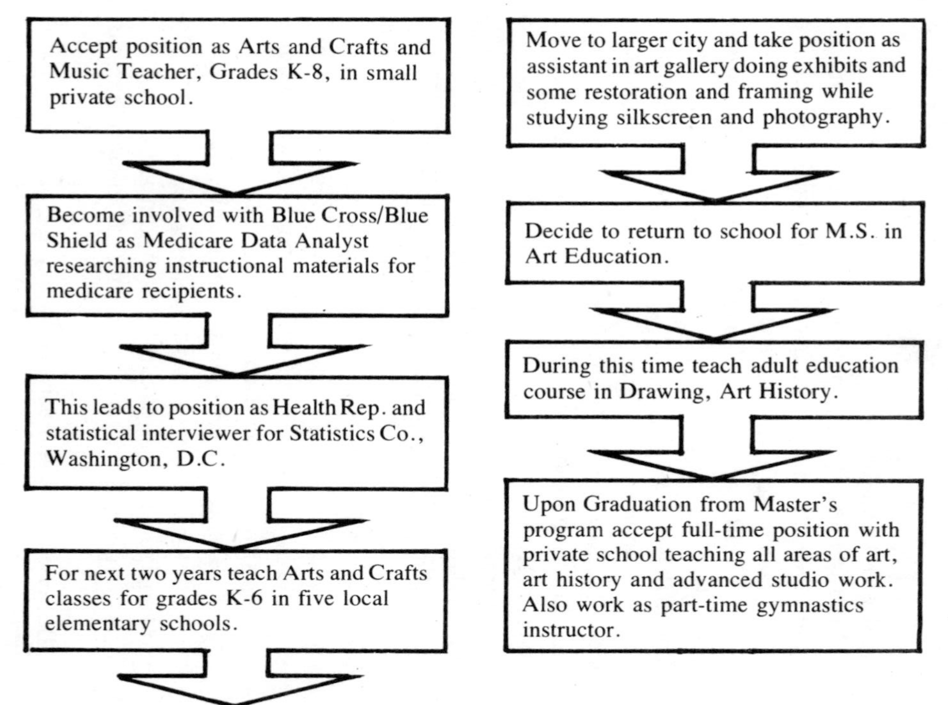

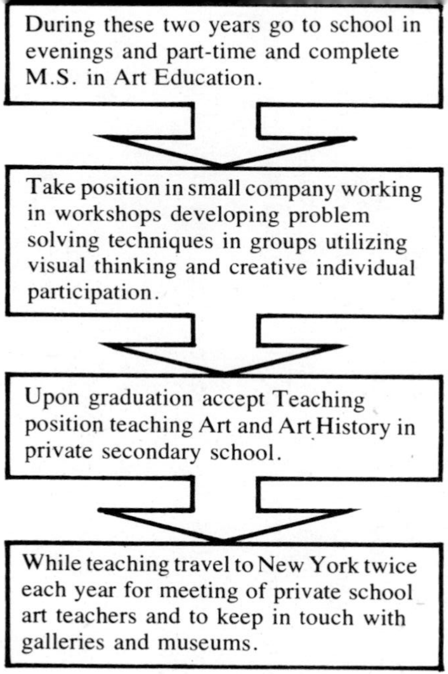

During these two years go to school in evenings and part-time and complete M.S. in Art Education.

Take position in small company working in workshops developing problem solving techniques in groups utilizing visual thinking and creative individual participation.

Upon graduation accept Teaching position teaching Art and Art History in private secondary school.

While teaching travel to New York twice each year for meeting of private school art teachers and to keep in touch with galleries and museums.

your resume and portfolio and continuing information will be available on position openings. The career planning office will assist you in the formation of your file of references, transcripts, resume, and will mail them to prospective employers. In preparing your dossier, you should request letters of recommendation from faculty who are familiar with your work as well as from cooperating teachers, principals, and others under whom you have worked or with whom you have had practice teaching.

You will follow the same principles for assembling a portfolio as described in Chapter XXII, but because you may want to include the work of the students you have had in practice teaching, be sure that it is clearly explained and readily identified as pupil work.

Education is ongoing, and you should make an effort to keep up with new and stimulating educational trends. Talk to fellow teachers and ask them about their experience in teaching. Much can be gained by frequent discussion with fellow educators and it helps you to be aware that your field is constantly broadening. Take part in new and innovative training programs offered by the Continuing Education Department of the college nearest you. You may want to participate in adult education programs and community offerings. You will be a much more interesting teacher for doing this, and you may find new directions for your career.

For those interested in college teaching, please read the chapter on fine arts.

CHAPTER XVII

Art Therapy

An art therapist is a person trained to use art in the field of rehabilitation. Those who may be rehabilitated include older people, younger people, rich people, poor people, people with emotional and physical dysfunctions.

The groundwork for art therapy was laid in the late 1930's. However, with the emphasis today being put on total mental health care, art therapy has become increasingly popular. The forming of the American Art Therapy Association has given new impetus to the profession and is now responsible for setting professional standards to be met by both artists and therapists. Art therapy is recognized and supported by psychiatrists and psychoanalysts as a primary method of treatment for emotionally disturbed patients. They agree that spontaneous expression tends to be more easily expressed in pictures than in words and is often a way for a patient to relieve deep-seated emotional problems.

Areas where art therapy is widely used include not only hospitals, but community mental health centers and schools for emotionally disturbed and brain damaged or physically handicapped children. It is also used in rehabilitation centers for drug addicts and alcoholics, and in prisons and other correctional institutions.

This field is growing in popularity as a career goal, and many schools and colleges are adding art therapy programs, electives, and options to their curriculum. If you are considering art

therapy as a career you should write to the American Art Therapy Association to express your interest. Ask for a list of schools offering accredited graduate and undergraduate programs. The Association may have suggestions on reading matter, books, or pamphlets, which would be helpful as an introduction to the field. Write to:

The American Art Therapy Association
3607 South Braeswood Boulevard
Houston, Texas 77025

Professional programs in this rapidly expanding field are directed towards providing students with specialized skills and training to enable them to work well in a variety of settings. If you are interested in entering art therapy, useful qualifications include a knowledge of, and some experience in, the techniques of art, drawing, painting, sculpture, and ceramics, as well as a basic knowledge of course work in the behavioral and social sciences. Because report writing is often necessary in a rehabilitation center, English and composition are important.

An undergraduate degree in Art Education will give you an excellent foundation on which to build a successful career in art therapy. It is also an option for many art and design undergraduate students who have enjoyed some experience in art therapy (perhaps as a volunteer in a mental health center) during their studies and want to become professionals in the field.

Art Therapy Career Paths

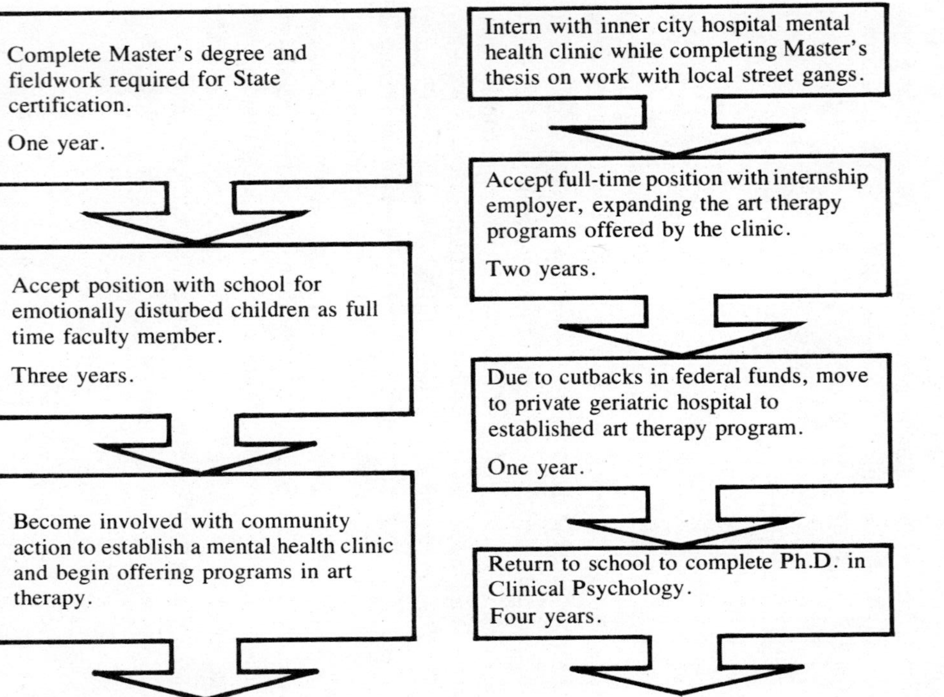

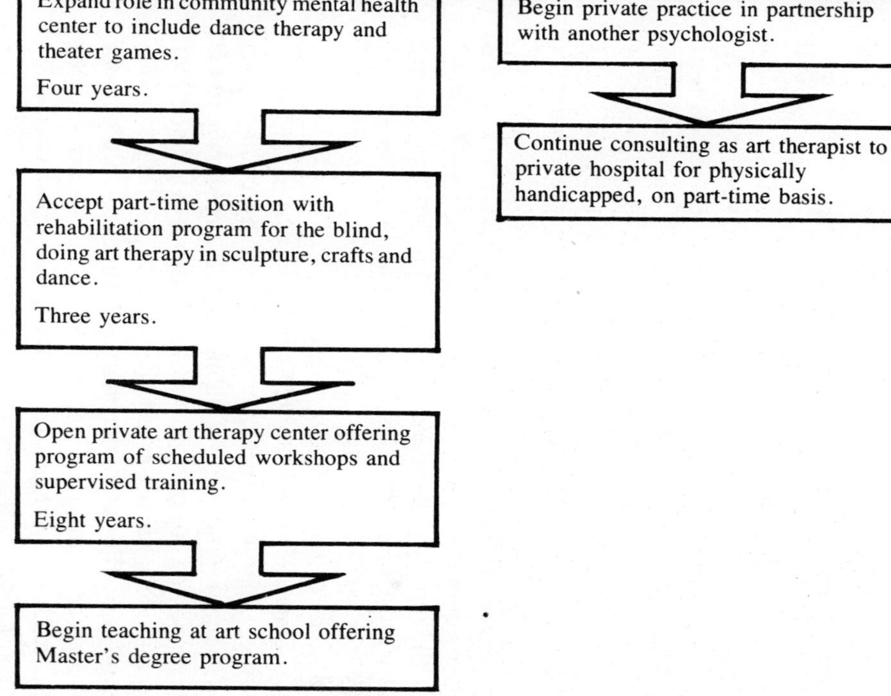
Expand role in community mental health center to include dance therapy and theater games.
Four years.
Accept part-time position with rehabilitation program for the blind, doing art therapy in sculpture, crafts and dance.
Three years.
Open private art therapy center offering program of scheduled workshops and supervised training.
Eight years.
Begin teaching at art school offering Master's degree program.
Begin private practice in partnership with another psychologist.
Continue consulting as art therapist to private hospital for physically handicapped, on part-time basis.

CHAPTER XVIII

Free-lancing

Free-lancing is the goal of both fine artists and designers, but as a way of life it is actually realized by very few. To be a free-lancer you must sell your art work and live independently of any designated employer. You are in a sense self-employed and your own administrator. You may use an artist's representative who will represent you to an employer for a fee, generally about 25 percent of the commission, but he/she will be demanding of your time, expect you to meet deadlines, and expect a full-time commitment on your part to produce work. However, "the rep" will be more aware of available opportunities and have greater interest in bigger commissions, which aids you both. Most free-lancers use "reps" and accept or reject the commissions as their success dictates.

To become a successful free-lancer you have to have a following. Your work becomes recognized by exhibiting in shows, being reproduced for publication, being shown on the screen, or having one or more well-known persons acclaim your talent. Suddenly you are asked to do several paintings, make a series of pots, film a documentary, illustrate a child's book, create a piece of furniture, or complete a special layout. One success leads to another, and you may even find yourself in business, hiring staff and keeping accounts.

As a free-lancer, one thing you must be very careful about is records. You will still have to pay bills, buy supplies, use the telephone, write some letters, and pay your taxes, probably on an estimated income basis as a self-employed individual. The

Internal Revenue Service is very particular about records and usually suggests you hire a certified public accountant whose business it is to know how to keep those records. When you are getting started as a free-lancer, the IRS can be very helpful in assisting you to set up a simple bookkeeping system before you are ready to hire an accountant.

Free-lancing seldom is for the beginner: First, because you do not have enough contacts and, second, because you do not have enough experience in your field, even though you may have had a number of jobs while in school. In the majority of cases, student free-lance jobs have supplemented other financial aid and have not been the sole means of support during student years. Exceptions, naturally, may prove the rule, but a mistake that is often made is that students who sell one piece of work think they are free-lancing. Nothing could be farther from the truth. Selling one piece of work will not support you, and selling successive pieces of work may be very difficult. Once you sell your work with relative ease, you are a free-lancer.

The advantages of being a successful free-lancer are: You may work when you choose (providing you meet your deadlines); you may accept the commissions you prefer; you may live where you choose (providing you have access to your clients and your work can be easily received by them); you are not responsible to an identifiable boss (you are he or she); and except for a rep's fee, if you have one, the money you make (after taxes) is your own to do with as you see fit.

The disadvantages are: uncertainty of continued work, increase in costs of supplies, necessity to maintain high quality work and a good reputation to keep clients satisfied, and the need to provide for yourself those benefits which include retirement and health insurance.

Knowing all this, there isn't a successful free-lancer anywhere who would have it any other way, and many of them supplement their incomes by adjunct teacher jobs, writing articles, and acting as consultants.

CHAPTER XIX

The Exploratory Interview

Once you have narrowed your career choice to one field within the many professional opportunities in art or design, you may want to use the exploratory interview technique to learn more about your career options. Most employers are willing to spend a reasonable amount of time with a young emerging professional. Your first task then is to identify firms specializing in your field or who employ professionals in your field with whom you would like to explore career opportunities. A call to the organization explaining your current status (as a student, recent graduate or young professional) and your desire to visit and learn more about what they do, and how their firm is organized, will usually get you an appointment at a mutually convenient time. Through this contact you can learn first hand how these professionals actually work.

In selecting individuals, firms, or design groups for exploratory interviews, you will probably want to choose a variety of potential work environments, small and large, corporate and government, as well as allied areas within your general field. For example, if you are in the communications area, you might want to explore a graphic design studio, a corporate graphic design department or advertising group, visit a free-lance illustrator, a TV station, a large advertising agency, or an industrial design consulting firm. Your goal will be to learn as much as you can about the "real world," how it works, and where you might fit in. Of course for this and any other type interview, you should familiarize yourself as much as possible with the work the firm or individual does through published material in periodicals and professional magazines. When you begin your actual job hunt, the contacts you have made during your exploratory interviews may offer assistance, referral to other resources, or even a job. You can use your own sensitivity in determining which of the people you meet react in a positive manner to you or your work if you bring your portfolio, and thus who may be willing to suggest possible contacts for employment. Finally, the exploratory interview is a career investigation tool which you may want to use some time before you are ready to seek full-time employment.

CHAPTER XX

How to Prepare a Resume

Your first introduction to many employers will be through your resume, and how you present yourself is extremely important. Because employers receive literally hundreds of resumes, yours should be concise and to the point—one page only for beginning job hunters—and geared to fit your particular major and choice of jobs. For instance, if you are interested in both teaching and non-teaching jobs, you prepare two resumes. You may do a special resume for a gallery, for admissions to graduate school, for summer and free-lance work, and for full-time jobs. You should not overdesign a resume, but you may add a special touch. The calligrapher may choose to letter a resume rather than type it; off-white or well-chosen colored paper may be used; a very brief resume may open like note paper with a wood cut or simple design or illustration on the front page and the facts printed inside on the second page. The contents of the resume are a brief description of your education and work experiences to date, including some shows and exhibits, but not every fair since junior high school.

The final draft of your resume is typewritten, and then can be taken to a printer to be reproduced by photo offset, a process whereby a picture is taken of the original and reproduced exactly as prepared, which means preparation is critical. This produces in the long run a less expensive and a more professional looking resume than one which has been photocopied.

Another method is to use press type headings or to have your entire resume typeset. You take your information, either handwritten or typewritten, to a printer who sets the type and with your approval prints the copy. In having your resume typeset, you have an opportunity to choose your typeface and to use different type for headings, for emphasis, and to differentiate. It makes your resume more original, but it is also more expensive.

However, the choice is yours, and the employer is really only going to be concerned with what you say and how you say it, but not with whether it is offset or typeset. Your goal is to attract the employer's attention with a well-designed presentation of your background and skills in a concise, well-edited format.

See examples which follow.

Boston, Massachusetts

Education: BFA Massachusetts College of Art 1976
Major: Illustration / Graphic Design
Four year Independent Study of Calligraphy

Experience: Illustrations for "Stockbridge Bicentennial Booklet" and "Boston Review of the Arts," 1975. Lettered brochure for "Millay Colony for the Arts", 1975, menus for "The Grand Hotel Curtis", Lenox, Massachusetts, numerous wedding, social and business invitations, "The Declaration of Interdependence for the Sheraton Corporation", 1976, certificates for The Childrens Hospital, Boston, the VFW in

Pittsfield, Massachusetts, and diplomas for Mass. College of Art, 1974, 75, 76. Designed lettered and painted signs for "The Curtis Hotel" and "Thistle Doo Plants", Stockbridge, plus many personalized free-lance work.

Exhibits: "Image Gallery", Stockbridge, Mass., May, 1975 and "Westernook Gallery", Sheffield, Mass., August, 1976.

Member: "The Christmas Store", Boston, an artist/craftsperson co-operative and The Southern Berkshire Community Arts Council, Monterey, Massachusetts.

OBJECTIVE

Graphic Design position requiring the ability to meet diverse graphic challenges with effective, contemporary design solutions.

EXPERIENCE

<u>Print</u>

Designed material of an institutional nature in the form of brochures, directories, posters and technical reports.

<u>Sound-Slide</u>

Designed and executed all visual aspects of various sound-slide programs for publicity and instructional purposes.
Developed visual concepts as criteria for programs let under contract.

<u>Overhead Projection</u>

Utilized latest Diazo techniques in the design and preparation of numerous transparency presentations.

<u>Exhibit/ Display</u>

Designed and directed fabrication of modular display units and exhibits for trade shows and publicity purposes. Directed assembly and lighting arrangements on location.

<u>Project Direction</u>

Initiated specifications and schedules for graphic projects let under contract. Reviewed for design proficiency and technical accuracy.

Provided concept and direction for various in-house design group projects.

EMPLOYMENT

U.S. Naval Training Device Center/ Port Washington, N.Y.
Visual Information Specialist (Feb. 1960 to present). Responsibilities correspond with preceding list of experience.

Earlier employment and free-lance assignments in advertising design relate to:

L.W. Frohlich, Intl. Advertising / New York City
Haines Advertising / Port Washington, New York
Design Directions / New York City
Williamsburg Publishing Co. / New York City
Snyder, Black and Schlegal / White Plains, New York
Resident Display / New York City

EDUCATION

Pratt Institute: Bachelor of Fine Arts degree in Advertising Design (Sept. 1955 to June 1959)

MILITARY

United States Marine Corps (July 1952 to July 1955)

PERSONAL

Age: 33 - Weight: 135 lbs. - Height: 5'7" - Married, two children

---

REFERENCES

Available on request

RESUME

experience	1/76-2/76	Proposed and taught at the Rhode Island School of Design, a photography course titled, "Altering the Silver Image," which dealt with various methods of applying color to black and white photographs.
	1/76-2/76	Supervised two students in Photography Independent Study Projects at the Rhode Island School of Design.
	9/75-12/75	As a Graduate Instructor, had full responsibility for teaching a R.I.S.D. undergraduate Photo Design course.
	9/74-6/75	As a Graduate Assistant, assisted another Graduate student with his teaching duties, and during R.I.S.D.'s Wintersession, assisted a full-time faculty member with an Intensive Fundamental Photography course.
	6/73-9/74	As an Instructor at The Clay People, a ceramics studio in Chicago, Illiinois, taught 2 classes, Intermediate and Advanced Stoneware Handbuilding Techniques.

	2/74–9/74	As an Assistant Photographer at Shigata-Wright Associates, a large commercial photo studio, had a wide range of responsibilities including studio lighting, set construction, exposure, processing and final presentation of finished color transparency materials.
	9/72–6/73	As a Teaching Assistant (a tuition-waiver, Work Scholarship position) at Columbia College, Chicago, Illinois, assisted in teaching beginning photography students basic black and white printing, negative development, print presentation, etc.
	10/67–2/72	As a Quality Assurance Anaylst for Johnson & Johnson Midwest Division, Chicago, Illinois, responsible for acceptance or rejection of incoming Raw Materials.
education	1976	M.F.A. Rhode Island School of Design, Providence Major Photography, elective work in Ceramics and Cinematography
	1973	B.A. Columbia College, Chicago, Illinois Major Photography, elective work in Ceramics, Printmaking and Fiction Writing
references		Available upon request

Experience

Drafting: Ability to draw mechanical assembly details, cross sections, orthographic and perspective views.

Model Making: Ability to work with wood, brass, plastic, plaster aluminum, putty, painting, and finishing.

Prototypes: Mastermold making with clay and plaster, prototype construction with polyester resin and fiberglass.

Photography: Photographing, developing and printing black and white film.

Illustration: Color pastel and marker, Prismatic pencil on Coloraid, tight work with Castell pen using stipple technique, several illustrations published in *Car & Driver*.

Creative Planning: Goal setting in relation to design problems and target dates for completion, attention to detail and followthrough.

Employment

12/74 to Present: Evans & Hillman, Horizon Design 251 Fifth Avenue N.Y.C. Preliminary lighting layout design, architectural model building.

7/74 to 9/74: Raymond Loewy/William Snaith,Inc. 110 E. 59th Street N.Y.C. Automotive planning, drafting, full-size mock-up layout and assembly.

6/73 to 9/73: Charles Pollock Associates Jackson Hgts. N.Y. Furniture design, drafting, model building, prototype construction and finishing.

Education

9/71 to Present: Pratt Institute Brooklyn, N.Y. June 1975 graduate, Bachelor of Industrial Design.

9/69 to 6/71: Delaware Technical & Community College Wilmington, Delaware. Associate Degree in Mechanical Engineering.

RESUME

Education	M.F.A. Painting, Rhode Island School of Design, Providence, RI - 1975
	B.A. Painting-Printmaking, State University College of New York at Potsdam, State University of New York at Buffalo - 1971
	State University College of New York at Buffalo, Summer Workshops - 1966
	Syracuse University, Summer Workshop - 1965
Professional Experience	Temporary Assistant Professor of Art, Marshall University, Huntington, West Virginia, Basic and Advanced Painting, Basic Design color and composition - 1975
	Instructor, Beginning and Advanced Painting, Summer session, Rhode Island School of Design - 1975
	Graduate Teaching Assistantship, Undergraduate Painting, Rhode Island School of Design - 1973-75
	Instructor, Advanced Painting, Summer session, Rhode Island School of Design - 1974
	Instructor of Visual Arts, Massena Central Schools, Massena, NY - 1972
	Instructor of Visual Arts, Hermon-DeKalk Central Schools, NY - 1971
	Assistant in Instruction, Chairman Painting Department, State University of New York at Potsdam - 1970
	Assistant in Instruction, Chairman Printmaking Department, State University College of New York at Potsdam - 1969

Courses Taught	Basic and Advanced Painting; Advanced Experimental Painting; Basic Design; Color and Composition; Advanced Drawing
Exhibitions and Group Shows	"16" contemporary Artists", Hartwick College, Oneonta, New York - 1975 Faculty Exhibition, Marshall University, Huntington Galleries, Huntington, West Virginia Graduate Thesis Exhibition, Museum of Art, Rhode Island School of Design - 1975 North Eastern Sculpture Association, Juried Exhibition, Brockton Art Center, Brockton, Massachusetts - 1975 Juried Painting Exhibition, Providence Art Club, Providence, RI - 1975 Group Exhibition, Woods-Gerry Gallery, Providence, Rhode Island - 1974 Group Exhibition, Newport Art Association, Newport, Rhode Island - 1973 New York State North Country Study Council Grant, Printmaking, Albany, New York - 1972 Juried Exhibition, Clarkson College of Technology, Potsdam, NY - 1971 Group Exhibition, State University College of New York at Potsdam - 1970 New York State Council on the Arts Juried Exhibition, Albany, NY - 1970 Participant, New York State Council on the Arts "Critic's Choice", New York, New York - 1969
Professional Organizations	College Art Association
References	Available upon request

INDUSTRIAL DESIGN

OBJECTIVE: To continue design work as a professional. Analysis and Development of conceptual design leading to a feasable solution for final design in terms of function, aesthetics, production and marketing factors.

EDUCATION: Massachusetts College of Art.
B.F.A. in Industrial Design. Emphasis on Product and Graphic Design, Interiors and Space Planning.

EMPLOYMENT:

Design Draftsman (Summer Employment)
Sheaffer Pen Company (Research Center)

Design Draftsman-Illustrator (Summer Employment)
Pro International Corporation, Dayton, Ohio.
Engineering and Concept Development Firm.
Patent and mechanical drafting. Techanical illustrating. Advertising layout and graphic design.

Consultant Designer/Company Treasurer of Partnership.
Probe, Dayton, Ohio. Industrial, Architectural, Graphic Design Studio.
Product development from concept to final product, including photographing and organizing and making presentation to client.

Staff Designer for Digital Equipment Corporation.
Designed numerous control consoles and panels including "Disk Pack Tester", " Dec Pack" disk memory storage unit. Responsible for several graphic layouts on company's newer equipment. Redesigned company's short cabinet enclosure. This consisted of alterations of both mechanical parts and visual appearance, introduction of new product color coordinated look, complete cost reduction in production of units also ability to be used as a modular & building block in conjunction with similar units.

Senior Designer on staff now consisting of 3 men. Responsible for complete major projects as well as contributing designer on minor projects. Responsible for face lift of PDP-10 large computer product line as well as contributing graphic designer for "Dec-System-10" new large computer system. Color coordinated whole product line as well as peripheral equipment used in conjunction with systems. Responsible for graphic layout and design of PDP-8M console computer. Contributed all graphics plus consol/bezel design for PDP-11/05 and PDP-11/03 minicomputer products. Responsible totally for "Dec-Data-System" office computer system. This consisted of responsibility as mechanical engineer, package designer, all graphic design, and supervisor responsible for first thirty pre-preduction-units. Contributing package designer for "RT-02", calculator, and "GT-40" graphic terminal. Proposed extruded packaging system now being incorporated. Established new graphic image now being used on systems. Consists of logo presentation, corporate-product image, and color landscaping. Designed graphics for company vehicles as well as for packaging.

Freelance Consultant Designer.
Design Interactions.
Halberts/Numa LTD. Kurz-Kasch Electronics Corp.
Monitor Corporation Riehl Electronics Corp.
Design interactions with clients have included product concept development, mechanical design, styling, graphics, and human factors intermixed with market familiarization, costing, production methods consideration, model building. Plus psychological and socialogical factors relating to the project. Corporate identity project. Advertising design and commercial art.

REFERENCES: Will be available on request.

CHAPTER XXI

How to Write a Letter of Application

If you apply for a job in writing, you will write a letter of application. How and what you write can mean the difference between being invited or not being invited for an interview. Since it is your first introduction to an employer, whether the letter of application is written inquiring about a specified job opening or to find out if there is an opening, you should take care in writing it. Essentially, be brief, be well-spoken, and be knowledgeable (see examples). A well-typewritten letter is always preferable unless you are a very good calligrapher and have the patience to write by hand. If you cannot type, find a friend who can or take typing as an elective (this goes for men and women alike). Every prospective employer should receive an original letter; never send a duplicated letter. Know to whom you are writing by name and title. A letter written to the art director or design department generally will never get past the secretary's desk; and in today's competitive market if you don't know who heads the department, you probably don't know too much about the department.

With your letter include your resume, which goes into more detail about your education and experience. Always sign your letter by pen and use your full name, not initials or nickname, unless you know the person to whom you are writing.

Remember employers receive far more letters than they read or respond to so do not be disappointed if you do not receive a reply. If you are writing to see if there is a job opening and do not receive a reply, the chances are there is no job opening. If you are writing in regard to a specific opening and refer properly to it, a well-presented letter usually receives a response.

Use simple stationery—unscented and unadorned and preferably white or non-color, like beige, ecru, light grey, oyster.

Lastly, if there is an organization in which you sincerely have an interest and do know something about their operation, you can write your letter accordingly. This kind of knowledge and sincerity are recognized and the follow through is often in your favor.

February 28, 1976

Mr. John O. Doe, Manager
Creative Division
Expressive Toys
Wagon Road
Providence, RI 02900

Dear Mr. Doe

In May, 1976, I will receive my Bachelor of Industrial Design degree and I will be looking for a position in which I can utilize my design education.

Because your firm has been involved in the manufacture of children's toys and my Degree project involved the creation of toys to develop children's perception and learning ability, I have a particular interest in becoming associated with an organization like Expressive Toys.

To give you a more descriptive background of my education and experience I enclose a resume and two slides of my completed project. I am available for a personal interview to which I will bring my portfolio; or if you prefer, I can mail a slide portfolio directly.

I hope I have the pleasure of hearing from you.

Sincerely,

February 28, 1977

Ms. Janet O. Doe, Director
Research and Design
Expressive Toys
Wagon Road
Providence, RI 02900

Dear Ms. Doe:

I have learned you have an opening for a designer/model maker and I am interested in applying.

In May, 1977, I will receive my Bachelor of Industrial Design degree; and during the last five years I have been a member of the Industrial Design Research Group. Involvement with this student group has included model-making for a table top project under a grant by Textron; production of prototypes for an Experimental Blood Collection System, and construction for a demonstration dwelling in an industrialized housing project.

To give you a more descriptive background of my education and experience, I enclose a resume and two slides of my completed project. I am available for a personal interview to which I will bring my portfolio; or if you prefer, I can mail a slide portfolio directly.

I hope I have the pleasure of hearing from you.

Sincerely,

February 28, 1976

Mr. John O. Doe, Manager
Creative Division
Expressive Toys
Wagon Road
Providence, RI 02900

Dear Mr. Doe:

I enjoyed our conversation on last Tuesday, and as you suggested I am writing a letter to give you a more complete background of my education and experience.

As indicated in my resume, my major course areas have included: design processes, methodology and research; human factors; modelmaking, furniture design; materials and production methods; photography; sketching, rendering and graphic techniques.

For the last three years, I have worked and gained professional experience as a member of a team which redesigned the weather presentation on Channel 10, WJAR, Providence; as a designer of furniture for perceptually deprived children under treatment in the Children's Perceptive Achievement Center; as a team member working on a study of sociological and technical implications on dining for Gorham Silver; as a researcher and designer for production of prototypes for an experimental blood collection system; as a construction worker for a demonstration dwelling in an industrialized housing project; as a fashion and copy work photographer for a New England department store.

I have had two pieces of work published in the *Industrial Design* magazine, November and December, 1975; in the *Providence Evening Bulletin;* and in the 1975 Rhode Island School of Design President's Report.

Under separate cover, I am having references forwarded to you, and my portfolio will be mailed within the next day or two.

I appreciate the time you have given to my presentation and I look forward to hearing from you and any suggestions you may have.

Sincerely yours,

CHAPTER XXII

How to Present a Portfolio

There is no short cut for the preparation of a professional portfolio. It is a long and tedious project which you should begin upon entering school and continue throughout your entire career. A portfolio is an uncompleted book constantly changing, but always up-to-date with new projects replacing old projects as your career progresses. Ideally, a portfolio should display a wide range of your talents, indicating creativity, innovation, and diversification. An effective portfolio should be self-explanatory, presenting your capabilities graphically and verbally integrated. If a design cannot be understood without explanation, it should be removed. The well-planned portfolio is capable of being mailed to or left with a client or employer. A portfolio should be didactic.

What Should Be Included in an Architecture Portfolio

(1) Completed projects
- (a) programs and titles
- (b) analyses
- (c) design sketches
- (d) presentation drawings
- (e) renderings
- (f) models
- (g) verbal explanations accompanying graphic plates

(2) Sketch problems
(3) Freehand sketches

(4) Renderings
(5) Working drawings
(6) Related interests: sculpture, painting, furniture design, creative photography, jewelry, ceramics, wood working, metalsmithing
(7) Resume

Keep the quality level of your portfolio consistent. Criticize yourself. Emphasize strong points and minimize weak ones. If, for example, you are a relatively poor renderer, don't include renderings. Be sensitive to your accomplishments.

What Should Be Included in an Art and Design Portfolio

The elements of a portfolio will vary with your chosen discipline. What you include will also depend on the type of position you are seeking. For example, a publisher seeking someone to do brochures will want to see primarily that kind of work. Below, in various categories, are suggested types of work to include:

GRAPHIC DESIGN
(1) Comps and/or printed work of graphic design concepts
(2) Roughs and finished art
(3) Sketches and drawings
(4) Illustrations
(5) Photography—also include photos used in design projects
(6) Lettering—comp lettering, calligraphy
(7) Typography
(8) Layouts
(9) Mechanicals
(10) Package design
(11) Related interests: exhibits, painting, sculpture
(12) Resume

INDUSTRIAL DESIGN

(1) Completed projects: rough sketches, renderings, drafting models, and verbal explanation
(2) Form and structure studies
(3) Rendering and presentation techniques
(4) Sketches
(5) Models
(6) Related interests: exhibits, paintings, sculpture
(7) Resume

COMMUNICATION DESIGN
(primarily book and publication design)

(1) Sketches and drawings (save sketch books)
(2) Illustrations
(3) Layouts
(4) Mechanicals and paste-ups
(5) Typography
(6) Photography—film
(7) Completed books: roughs and limited edition versions
(8) Related interests: exhibits, painting, sculpture
(9) Resume

You may want to present a more specialized portfolio with specific examples of your area of interest, such as photography, illustration, graphic design, film, package design. If so, take special care to include a broad variety of work, showing different concepts, purposes, and techniques within your field. Special attention should be given to presentation and preparation when your work is primarily three-dimensional or when you are preparing a film portfolio.

A design portfolio should consist of approximately 15-30 pieces (depending on size) of your best work selected from the categories given above.

Format and Binding

One of the first decisions in preparation of a portfolio is format. Some standard paper formats are: 8″ × 10″, 11″ × 14″, 14″ × 17″, and 16″ × 20″. However, there is no need to feel limited. It is possible to utilize a non-standard format if it will more effectively present your designs. The portfolio pages should be used either horizontally or vertically so they can be viewed consistently. The material of which the page is made may be one of many: photographic paper, mat board, colored construction paper, bristol board, foam core. Consideration should be given to the overall weight and convenience in handling when choosing mounting or backing materials. The choice of format and page material dictates the method of binding. If you use standard formats, you have available standard leather and vinyl portfolios and standard acetate leaves. If you wish to utilize a non-standard format, you must suitably bind your portfolios yourself or place your work neatly in an attaché-type portfolio. The non-standard format portfolio is obviously more difficult to design and construct. However, the final product may be well worth the extra effort. The acetate loose-leaf spiral bound portfolio is recommended primarily because of its flexibility. You can easily rearrange your work, adding and subtracting as you progress or change your career goals.

Method of Presentation

The methods of presentation depend on three things: (1) the work to be presented; (2) the reproduction techniques available; and (3) the budget. Sometimes cost is only one consideration. The reproductive media available are listed below in order of decreasing cost.

(1) Photographic print (color), at least 5″ × 7″

(2) Color transparency (color, 35mm or 2; the latter is recommended)
(3) Photographic prints (black and white)
(4) Photostat (black and white)
(5) Blue print, brown line, blue line, sepia, etc.

Examples of reproductive media used in specific situations:

(1) Drawings: color print, color slides, B & W print, photostat
(2) Models: color print, color slides, B & W print
(3) Drafting and working drawings: photostat, blue line, black line, white line, sepia
(4) Lettering: photostat, negative or positive
(5) Package and graphic comps: color print, color slides
(6) Layouts: photostat, blue line, black line

To make a more interesting presentation, the plates in a portfolio may be different in reproduction technique. In addition, choice of the reproduction technique can reduce an overly large presentation to the size of your portfolio. The choice of media should include some examples of original work, except when you are seeking employment out of your current locale. In this case you will probably prefer to prepare a portfolio of carefully marked slides.

Page Composition

The use of the "page" in the portfolio depends on your choice of format. However, the relationship of one plate to the next and the individual page composition should be considered carefully. If you are using an acetate loose-leaf binder, you have the opportunity to create a comprehensive layout thoughout. By using both sides of each page, you can produce a book with added continuity.

Color

Judicious introduction of color into a basically black and white portfolio can add life to an otherwise dull presentation. Several ways of adding color are:

(1) Color originals
(2) Color photographs
(3) Color backing sheets
(4) Color page inserts
(5) Color magic marker added to black and white prints, photostats, blue lines, brown lines
(6) Tissue paper or colored zip-a-tone added to blue lines, black lines, sepias
(7) Color graphics

Three-Dimensional Work

Unless a project is relatively small, three-dimensional work must be presented in either photographs or slides for convenience of transportation. An exception might by the inclusion of a small model in a specialized portfolio.

Verbal Explanation

Every portfolio, particularly in the areas of architecture and graphic and industrial design, should include verbal explanation. All work presented should be titled and preferably accompanied by a brief description of concepts, aims, goals. The actual writing may be hand-lettered, typed, or presented in transfer lettering.

Conclusion

Remember, your portfolio speaks for you. Present only your own work or indicate what your contribution was on a printed piece. Use your imagination and abilities to create an attractive and honest presentation of your talents, and accompany your portfolio with a resume. (See Chapter XX.)

CHAPTER XXIII

How to Make the Final Decision

An important moment is at hand. You are offered a job, and with the exception of those part-time jobs you had while going to school, this is your first full-time professional job. Should you accept it? Before making a decision, here are some things to keep in mind.

1. Hopefully you have had a personal interview, have visited the organization, and have met the other employees so that you know the kinds of people with whom you will be working and the kinds of conditions under which you will work. Salary and salary goals should have been discussed, and you should have a positive feeling about the assignment.

2. Remember, a first job is a first job. No more. It is not a lifetime commitment, although the desire to be an artist or designer may be.

3. On the other hand, even on a first job it is unfair to you and the employer if you take the job for no more than three or four months. For a job to have any value, a year appears a minimum amount of time, unless there are truly extenuating circumstances.

4. If the job appears to be one where you will gain good experience, you may want to stay as long as three years. After three years, however, you will want to ask yourself, "What are

my long-term goals and what does staying here mean to my future?"

5. If your job future means getting additional education, an important decision will be earning enough money to pursue this course and perhaps bringing with you to graduate school sufficient skills to help you get an assistantship.

6. Whatever the job, you will want to keep an up-to-date portfolio and an available resume to be ready for the next step, be it a better job or more schooling.

An important decision may be your job versus your goals. From time to time creative people get into positions where their talents are rewarded by promotion which takes them out of the creative arts area and into the responsibilities of administration. When this happens, a certain frustration can ensue and a decision has to be made—to remain or not remain as a working artist. You can, of course, become an after-hours artist, and there are those who do so very successfully, but you may find this difficult and feel you are losing touch with your original intentions.

Only you can make this decision. But whatever you decide, working carries with it a responsibility to respect yourself, your profession, and the people with whom you are working. A sense of dedication and integrity creates an atmosphere where more will be accomplished and more personal satisfaction will be achieved. A balanced sense of humor keeps frustration down and creativity up. With these combinations, decision making becomes easier and closer to the mark.

CHAPTER XXIV

Business Procedures, Law, and Taxes

The legal problems which beset the artist are many and of infinite variety, and it would be inappropriate to ignore them. It is impossible to cover this subject adequately in one chapter because it has been done well in other publications, which are listed below and which will be of use to the artist as well as the lawyer, if one is called in to solve a legal problem. Problems may be in the area of production, marketing, ownership, display, authentication, or preservation of works of art. Among some of the solutions covered are the tax problems which may arise for the artist when he attempts to support himself through the creation of his work, whether in painting, drawing, graphic design, sculpture, photography, or film. Of course, if a really serious problem arises, the artist should seek legal advice either through his own lawyer or by taking advantage of one of the numerous available volunteer lawyers who give this kind of service. If you write to The Artists Equity Association, 2813 Albemarle Street, S.W., Washington, D.C., you can ask for the address of the association nearest to you. For a list write to: Volunteer Lawyers for the Arts, 1564 Broadway, New York, N.Y. 10036.

The above are but two of the growing number of organizations formed for the express purpose of providing assistance to the artist. We also note that the Second Edition of *The Artists Reserved Rights Transfer and Sale Agreement* is now available. This new edition is much shorter and less difficult to read and to use, and may be obtained by writing to Artists Rights Association, 27 West 15th Street, New York, N.Y. 10011.

The growing interest in the law and legality pertaining to art is the result of the growing dignity and importance of art and visual communication during the last twenty years and the artist's demand for full and equal rights with all other fields of endeavor.

Listed below are a number of books available which give good advice and information on several areas of business procedures and law and taxes for the visual artist:

Legal & Business Problems of Artists, Art Galleries, and Museums, by Franklin Feldman and Stephen Weil. Published by Practicing Law Institute.

The Sale of Works of Art, by Geraldine Keen. Published by Nelson.

Arts and Crafts Service. Published Business Information for Craftsmen by the State Department of Education, Montpelier, VT 05602.

The American Artist Business Letter, published by American Artist, 2160 Patterson Street, Cincinnati, OH 45214. This is a monthly updating of legal issues brought to the attention of the editors by readers. It answers readers' questions and gives examples of situations. Most valuable.

Architectural Practice and Procedure, by Hamilton Turner. Published by B. T. Batsford, Ltd. This would be a good tool for the industrial designer as well as for the architect and interior designer.

The Copyright Handbook for Fine & Applied Arts, by Howard Walls. Published by Watson-Guptill. This has been planned to give a broad and comprehensive knowledge of the ins and outs of copyright.

Business & the Arts—An Answer to Tomorrow, by Arnold Gingrich. Published by Eriksson.

Art Works, Law, Policy, Practice, by Franklin Feldman and Stephen Weil. Published by Practicing Law Institute. One of the most thorough and comprehensive books involving American law as it relates to art work.

The Visual Artist and the Law, by Associated Councils of the Arts, The Association of the Bar of the City of New York, Volunteer Lawyers for the Arts. This book informs the artist of significant legal problems and the solutions which might be possible.

What Every Artist & Collector Should Know About the Law, by Scott Hodes. Published by E. P. Dutton & Co., Inc. Designed for the layman, it explores some of the legal ramifications involved in being an artist, photographer, dealer, collector, or museum coordinator.

Art & the Law, by Howard Thorkelson. Published by The Volunteer Lawyers for the Arts in New York City. Note that an excellent brief description of the copyright law is contained in the pamphlet, "Copyright in Works of Art," by Joshua Cahn for Artists Equity.

Tax problems of the artist are well taken care of in a simple, easy to follow book, *The Visual Artist and the Law.* The chapter on "Tax Problems of the Artist" deals with the effect of three federal taxes: income tax, gift tax, and estate tax. It is noted that the Internal Revenue Service has its own advisory panel with respect to art valuation. This panel is composed of art dealers, museum curators, and art educators who advise the IRS on art valuation questions. Therefore, it might be well to consult the IRS if any question arises not answered in one of the books listed above.

If the artist has questions about social security, answers may be obtained from any local office of the Department of Health, Education, and Welfare or by consulting a lawyer.

Reading List

AMERICAN ARCHITECTS DIRECTORY
R. R. Bowker Company
1180 Avenue of the Americas
New York, N.Y. 10036

AMERICAN ART DIRECTORY
R. R. Bowker Company
1180 Avenue of the Americas
New York, N.Y. 10036

THE 53rd ANNUAL OF ADVERTISING—THE ONE SHOW
Print
6400 Goldsboro Road
Washington, D.C. 20034

52nd ANNUAL OF ADVERTISING, EDITORIAL & TELEVISION ART & DESIGN
Watson-Guptill Publications
165 West 46th Street
New York, N.Y. 10036

ARCHITECTURAL SCHOOLS OF NORTH AMERICA
The Association of Collegiate Schools of Architecture
1735 New York Avenue, N.W.
Washington, D.C. 20006

53rd ART DIRECTOR'S ANNUAL
Print
6400 Goldsboro Road
Washington, D.C. 20034

ART DIRECTOR'S HANDBOOK—EUROPE
Peter Glenn Publications, Inc.
145 East 53rd Street
New York, N.Y. 10022

ART WORKS, LAW, POLICY PRACTICE
Practising Law Institute
810 Seventh Avenue
New York, N.Y. 10019

ARTIST MARKET
9933 Alliance Road
Cincinnati, Ohio 45242

THE ARTIST'S GUIDE TO HIS MARKET
Watson-Guptill Publications
165 West 46th Street
New York, N.Y. 10036

AUDIOVISUAL MARKET PLACE
R. R. Bowker Company
1180 Avenue of the Americas
New York, N.Y. 10036

COMPUTER GRAPHICS/COMPUTER ART
College Art Association
16 East 52nd Street
New York, N.Y. 10022

CONTEMPORARY CRAFTS MARKET PLACE
R. R. Bowker
P.O. Box 1807
Ann Arbor, Michigan 48106

CRAFTS ANNUAL
Publishing Center for Cultural Resources
27 West 53rd Street
New York, N.Y. 10019

THE CREATIVE BLACK BOOK
Universe Publishing Company
381 Park Avenue
New York, N.Y. 10016

DIRECTORY OF ACCREDITED SUMMER CAMPS
American Camping Association
Bradford Woods
Martinsville, Indiana 46151

DIRECTORY OF ALTERNATIVE SCHOOLS
The New Schools Exchange
P.O. Box 820
St. Paris, Ohio 43072

DIRECTORY OF THE ASSOCIATION OF AMERICAN UNIVERSITY PRESSES, INC.
The Association of American University Presses, Inc.
One Park Avenue
New York, N.Y. 10016

DIRECTORY OF POSTSECONDARY SCHOOLS WITH OCCUPATIONAL PROGRAMS
Superintendent of Documents
U.S. Government Printing Office
Washington, D.C. 20402

FINE ARTS MARKET PLACE
R. R. Bowker Company
P.O. Box 1807
Ann Arbor, Michigan 48106

GEBBIE HOUSE MAGAZINE DIRECTORY
National Research Bureau
424 Third Street
Burlington, Iowa 53601

GO HIRE YOURSELF AN EMPLOYER
Anchor Books
Anchor Press, Doubleday
Garden City, N.Y. 11530

GRADUATE AND PROFESSIONAL SCHOOL OPPORTUNITIES FOR MINORITY STUDENTS
Educational Testing Service
Princeton, N.J. 08540

GRADUATE PROGRAMS AND ADMISSIONS MANUAL . . Volume B, Arts and Humanities
Educational Testing Service
Princeton, N.J. 08540

GRANTS AND AID TO INDIVIDUALS IN THE ARTS
Washington International Arts Letter
115 5th Street, S.E.
Washington, D.C. 20003

THE GRANTS REGISTER
St. Martin's Press
175 Fifth Avenue
New York, N.Y. 10010

GUIDE TO FINANCIAL AIDS AVAILABLE TO STUDENTS IN ARTS & SCIENCES
Compiled by the Office of Career Plans & Placement
State University of New York at Binghamton
Binghamton, N.Y. 13901

GUIDE TO STUDY IN GREAT BRITAIN
Study in Britain Association
66 Banbury Road
Oxford, OX2 6PR, England

HOME FURNISHINGS—INFORMATION BOOK
National Home Fashion League
15043 Califa Street
Van Nuys, California 91401

HOW TO GET A JOB OVERSEAS
Arco Publishing Company
219 Park Avenue South
New York, N.Y. 10003

HOW TO MAKE A LIVING AS A PAINTER
Watson-Guptill Publications
165 West 46th Street
New York, N.Y. 10036

LITERARY MARKET PLACE
R. R. Bowker Company
1180 Avenue of the Americas
New York, N.Y. 10036

MADISON AVENUE HANDBOOK
Peter Glenn Publications, Ltd.
19 East 48th Street
New York, N.Y. 10017

MUSEUM TRAINING COURSES IN THE U.S. AND CANADA
American Association of Museums
2233 Wisconsin Avenue. N.W.
Washington, D.C. 20007

NATIONAL ASSOCIATION OF SCHOOLS OF ART DIRECTORY
National Association of Schools of Art
11250 Roger Bacon Drive, #5
Reston, Virginia 22070

NEW YORK CITY RESOURCES FOR THE ARTS AND ARTISTS
Cultural Council Foundation
41 East 65th Street
New York, N.Y. 10021

OCCUPATIONAL HANDBOOK FOR COLLEGE GRADUATES
U.S. Department of Labor
Washington, D.C. 20402

OFFICIAL HANDBOOK—MOTION PICTURE, TV, AND THEATRE DIRECTORY
Motion Pictures Enterprises Publications, Inc.
Tarrytown, N.Y. 10591

THE OFFICIAL MUSEUM DIRECTORY
The American Association of Museums
2233 Wisconsin Avenue, N.W.
Washington, D.C. 20007

THE PAINTER'S DICTIONARY OF MATERIALS AND METHODS
Watson-Guptill Publications
165 West 46th Street
New York, N.Y. 10036

PHOTOGRAPHY MARKET PLACE
R. R. Bowker Company
1180 Avenue of the Americas
New York, N.Y. 10036

PHOTOGRAPHY—SOURCE & RESOURCE
Light Impressions
P.O. Box 3012
Rochester, N.Y. 14614

PRICING AND ETHICAL GUIDELINES FOR ILLUSTRATORS AND DESIGNERS
Graphic Artist Guild
407 East 77th Street
New York, N.Y. 10021

PRIVATE FOUNDATIONS ACTIVE IN THE ARTS, VOLUME TWO
Washington International Arts Letter
P.O. Box 90005
Washington, D.C. 20003

PRIVATE SCHOOLS
Porter Sargent
11 Beacon Street
Boston, Massachusetts 02108

REQUIREMENTS FOR CERTIFICATION
University of Chicago Press
Chicago, Illinois 60637

SCHOOLS ABROAD
Porter Sargent
11 Beacon Street
Boston, Massachusetts 02108

STANDARD DIRECTORY OF ADVERTISING AGENCIES
National Register Publishing Company, Inc.
5201 Old Orchard Road
Skokie, Illinois 60076

STUDY ABROAD
Institute of International Education
809 United Nations Plaza
New York, N.Y. 10017

STUDY ABROAD
International Scholarships & Courses
UNESCO
Place de Fontenoy
75 Paris–7e

SUMMER EMPLOYMENT DIRECTORY
National Directory Service
266 Ludlow Avenue
Cincinnati, Ohio 45220

TEACHING ABROAD
Unipub, Inc.
P.O. Box 433
New York, N.Y. 10016

U.S. SPONSORED PROGRAMS ABROAD
Unipub, Inc.
P.O. Box 433
New York, N.Y. 10016

VIDEO RESOURCES IN NEW YORK STATE
Publishing Center for Cultural Resources
27 West 53rd Street
New York, N.Y. 10019

WHOLE WORLD HANDBOOK
Council on International Educational Exchange
777 United Nations Plaza
New York, N.Y. 10017

WORLD-WIDE SUMMER EMPLOYMENT DIRECTORY
The Advancement and Placement Institute
169 North 9th Street
Brooklyn, N.Y. 11211

Publications

Advocates for the Arts, Associated Councils of the Arts, 1564 Broadway, Suite 820, New York, N.Y. 10036.

American Artist, 1 Color Court, Marion, Ohio 43302.

American Artist Business Letter, 2160 Patterson Street, Cincinnati, Ohio 45214.

Architectural Digest, P. O. Box 2418, Boulder, Colorado 80302.

Art in America, 115 Tenth Street, Des Moines, Iowa 50301.

The Art Bulletin, College Art Association of America, 432 Park Avenue South, New York, N.Y. 10016.

Art Journal, College Art Association of America, 432 Park Avenue South, New York, N.Y. 10016

The Art Letter, 150 East 58th Street, New York, N.Y. 10022.

Art News, 121 Garden Street, Marion, Ohio 43302.

Art Workers News, National Art Workers Community, 32 Union Square East, New York, N.Y. 10003.

Arts, Inc., Box 32382, Washington, D.C. 20007—Newsletter for job referral in the Visual and Performing Arts.

Bulletin for Film and Video Information, 80 Wooster Street, New York, N.Y. 10012.

Communications Arts Magazine, P. O. Box 10300, Palo Alto, California 94303.

Craft Horizons, Craft Horizons of America, Crafts Council, 44 West 53rd St., New York, N.Y. 10019.

Design and Environment, 6400 Goldsboro Road, N. W., Washington, D.C. 20034.

Design Magazine, London, England.

Federal Design Matters, Superintendent of Documents, Public Documents Department, U. S. Government Printing Office, Washington, D.C. 20402.

The Feminist Art Journal, 41 Montgomery Place, Brooklyn, N.Y. 11215.

Industrial Design, P. O. Box 2153, Radnor, Pennsylvania 19089.

New England Advertising Week, Editor and Printer Publishing Company, 470 Atlantic Avenue, Boston, Massachusetts 02210.

Packaging Design, 6400 Goldsboro Road, N. W., Washington, D.C. 20034.

Print, 6400 Goldsboro Road, N. W., Washington, D.C. 20034.

Smithsonian, Smithsonian Institution, 1255 Portland Place, Boulder, Colorado 80302.

Sunshine Artists, Sun Country Enterprise, Inc., P. O. Box 426, Fern Park, Florida 32730.

Vogue Magazine, Conde Nast Publications, Inc., 420 Lexington Avenue, New York, N.Y. 10017.

Washington International Arts Letter, Capitol Hill, 115 5th Street, S. E., Washington, D.C. 20003.

Women's Wear Daily, 7 East 12th Street, New York, N.Y. 10003.

Index